FEELINGS AND EMOTIONS
IN
CHRISTIAN LIVING

FEELINGS AND EMOTIONS IN CHRISTIAN LIVING

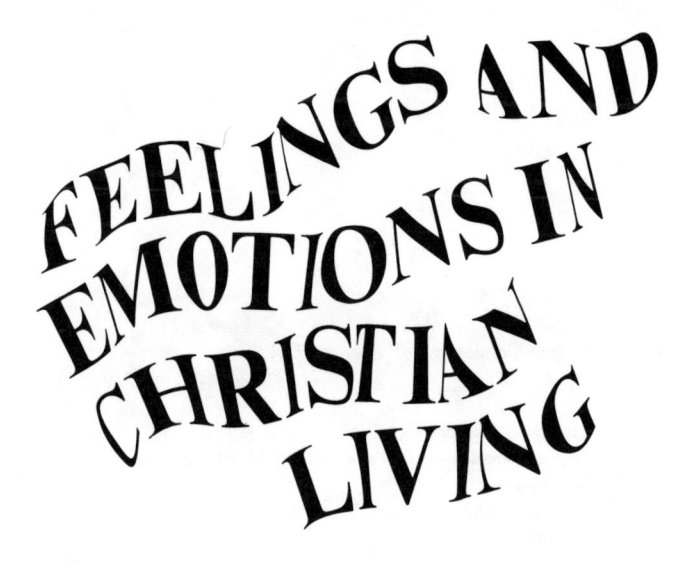

Mary Michael O'Shaughnessy, OP

ALBA · HOUSE   NEW · YORK

SOCIETY OF ST. PAUL, 2187 VICTORY BLVD., STATEN ISLAND, NEW YORK 10314

Library of Congress Cataloging-in-Publication Data

O'Shaughnessy, Mary Michael.
    Feelings and emotions in Christian living / Mary Michael
O'Shaughnessy.
        p. xiii + 152   cm. 14 × 21.
    Bibliography: p.
    ISBN 0-8189-0524-7
    1. Christian life — Catholic authors.   2. Emotions — Religious
aspects — Christianity.   I.   Title.
BX2350.2.078   1988
248.4'82 — dc 19   87-21317
                                                                                   CIP

Designed, printed and bound in the United States of
America by the Fathers and Brothers of the
Society of St. Paul, 2187 Victory Boulevard,
Staten Island, New York 10314, as part of their
communications apostolate.

---

2 3 4 5 6 7 8 9 (Current Printing: first digit)

© Copyright 1988 by the Society of St. Paul

DEDICATION

*To the memory
of my mother and father*
Lurline A. Linden and Arthur O'Shaughnessy

ACKNOWLEDGMENTS

I AM GRATEFUL to the Cenacle Retreat House in St. Louis for asking me to prepare and present a prayer/study week-end on "Feelings and Emotions in Christian Living." Since then I have shared this material with numerous groups in conference centers and retreat houses around the country. I have learned much from the people who participated in these week-end sessions; so much so that I have continually modified, changed, and enhanced the material that I originally presented. Then I started with a clear broth; now I have a thick gumbo to share with others.

Specific persons have been both supporters and enablers for me: Sister Mary Edmund Gibson, O.P., the present major superior, who upon my request, provided me with optimum living and working space in order to put my thoughts on paper and with the appropriate materials (a personal computer and printer) to facilitate the writing; and Sister Mary Louise Albrecht, O.P. who read the entire manuscript and made invaluable suggestions which improved the clarity and precision of both the writing style and the content of each chapter.

TABLE OF CONTENTS

Introduction	xi
Chapter One: *Human Emotion and Christian Living*	
Introduction	3
The Mystery of Human Personhood	4
Experiencing Feeling and Emotion	6
Expressing Feeling and Emotion	9
Adult Responsibility and Feeling and Emotional Behavior	13
Abba-God and Feelings and Emotions	15
Summary	16
Chapter Two: *Gladness, Life-Delight, Joy and Pleasure*	
Introduction	21
Our Capacity for Joy	22
Strategies for Joy	23
Summary	36
Chapter Three: *Sadness and Grief, Mourning and Loss*	
Introduction	41
Our Experience of Death — Sadness and Grief	42
Our Experience of Other Death Events	46
Our Inner Death Experiences	50
Our Unreal Expectations for Others	53
Our Response to the Unreal Expectations of Others	56
Unreal Expectations that We Impose upon Ourselves	58

Our Expressions of Sadness, Grief and Loss 60
Summary 63

Chapter Four: *Anger and Christian Integrity*
Introduction 67
Our Experiences of Anger 69
Our Expressions of Anger 70
Strategies for Expressing our Anger in a
    Mature Manner 73
Anger and our Christian Life 76
Summary 82

Chapter Five: *Anger — Its Many Faces and Expressions*
Introduction 87
Depression 87
Passive Aggression 91
Jealousy, Envy and Resentment 94
Sarcasm and Dark Humor 98
Hurt, Forgiveness and Reconciliation 99
Summary 102

Chapter Six: *Fear — Healthy and Unhealthy*
Introduction 107
Our Experience of Fear 108
Sacred Scripture and Fear 116
Summary 122

Chapter Seven: *Fear Imaging and Faith Imaging*
Introduction 129
Three Issues of Fear 130
Fear Imaging 136
Faith Imaging 139
Faith Imaging and Sacred Scripture 143
Summary 146

Bibliography 151

INTRODUCTION

SOME TIME BACK, Sister Sally Towne, R.C., then in ministry at the Cenacle Retreat House in St. Louis, asked me to present a weekend on "Feelings and Emotions" for Christian adults interested in the impact of feelings and emotions upon their spiritual growth and development. These women and men were concerned about the correlation and the integration of their affective behavior with the Gospel message and the affective impact of the Christ event upon them in today's milieu. They were interested in discovering how adult Gospel living and mature emotional behavior are interrelated. In the process of my preparation for the material for the prayer/study weekend, I concentrated on the four basic feelings and emotions which influence our behavior both as human beings and as Christian women and men — joy or life-delight, grief over loss, anger, and fear. These four feelings and emotional experiences are also frequently apparent in the lives of the women and men of the Scriptures. Central to my preparation was the awareness that we Westerners tend to think with our heads and to feel with our hearts; whereas the Semitic people in the Scriptures tended to think with their hearts and to feel with their guts or bowels. So it is that the significance of the Scriptures can be elusive to someone who expects to obtain meaning and wisdom *only* through a logical or intellectual process. Both the Hebrew and the Christian Scriptures speak to the *whole* person, not merely to the intellect, and thus demand openness and receptivity from the emotions as well as from the deepest recesses of our being.

My purpose in exploring and presenting my observations is to indicate strongly the *central* role of our affective life in living the Christian life as adult women or men. We cannot expect to live the Christian life as mature women and men of the Gospel without doing our homework in clearing away, cleaning out, and re-framing some of our emotional positions and postures regarding ourselves, others, and *Abba*-God. In reality our feelings and emotions function as filters. They continually sift both the awareness coming into our consciousness from persons and situations in our environment and from the awareness which emerges from within us, from the depths of our personhood. Moreover, both psychology and Christian spirituality are disciplines which focus in upon human behavior, upon behavioral patterns which can be constructive or destructive, liberating or enslaving, life-giving or death-dealing both for ourselves and for others. Another dimension which needs to be examined is how we are able to convert the destructive side of some of our negative feelings and emotions into constructive processes. Grief, anger, and fear have some very life-giving powers to bestow upon each of us; the positive feelings and emotions of joy and life-delight also possess destructive energies which we need to control and discipline. I perceive sound psychological theory and sound Scriptural theology as mutually receptive and compatible with each other. Thomas Aquinas' dictum, *Grace builds on nature*, is very appropriate in this mutuality of focus — human personhood — which both psychology and Scriptural theology enjoy.

There are some personal preferences in this text to which I need to alert my reader:

1) Most of my references to the God of Jesus Christ will read *Abba*-God. I employ this title which Jesus of Nazareth

used in his prayer to call attention to the relationship with God which Jesus inaugurated for us. The title, *Abba*-God, is in contrast to the Yahweh and Elohim titles found in the Hebrew Scriptures. *Abba*-God expresses a *Child's* relationship with God; it is an intimate, spontaneous, trusting, joyful relationship with God. The Hebrew word, *Abba*, means *Daddy* or *Papa* — hence, *Daddy*-God or *Papa*-God.

2) Practically all of my references to the two Testaments in the Scriptures will read Hebrew and Christian rather than the Old and the New Testaments. In reality the Old is always new for us in terms of its impact, meaning, and significance for our Christian lives. The frequent use of the Hebrew Scriptures in our Christian liturgy amply indicates their value and importance for us today.

3) My use of the terms "feelings" and "emotions" are not interchangeable. For me, the term "feelings" indicates a more surface and a less profound inner experience of a given affective awareness than the term "emotion" does.

ONE

Human Emotion And Christian Living

INTRODUCTION

HUMAN FEELING AND EMOTION are central to the daily drama of Christian living, especially the drama of religious experience. Each human life is a profoundly poignant drama — at times, both tragic and comic. The interplay of forces, controlled and uncontrolled, in each human life creates an impact of personal and social meaning that dramatists throughout the centuries, have struggled to penetrate and to present with accuracy, beauty, and power. And human feeling and emotion are interwoven inextricably in the life fabric of each human individual. Joy and delight, sadness and hurt, anger and hostility, fear and anxiety, guilt and shame — each colorful thread weaves its passage in and out of the tapestry of our personal and social life. Feelings and emotions color and create the texture and form of our individual drama in our unique time and space, in our social milieu.

The word "emotion" comes from the Latin, *e(x)-movere* which means to move out, to agitate, to stir up, to excite, to arouse, to disturb. The meaning of the word presupposes human centeredness and interiority. Deep within, each one of us is called to deal with disturbance, interruption, and agitation. The word "feeling" comes from the Old English, *felan* which conveys sensory awareness in terms of the tactile — touching and being touched. In the broader sense it includes one's ability to experience emotion (to be touched) and to be open to sensation, to be receptive to sensory impressions, to be sensitive to impinging reality. Again, the meaning of the word affirms human subjectivity, human centeredness, and human interiority in relation to self and the environment. In everyday parlance, people with whom we relate are described in terms of their affective sensibility: "hard as a rock," "cold as steel," "narrow as baby ribbon," "closed as a clam," "open as a book," "sharp as a tack." So it is that we easily articulate our perceptions of others with these and other capsuled images.

THE MYSTERY OF HUMAN PERSONHOOD

EACH OF US participates in the Mystery of *Abba*-God, the God of Jesus Christ. Each of us is created by *Abba*-God with inner beauty and power. Each of us is re-created by Jesus Christ in the Spirit. Daughters and sons of *Abba*-God are we! Sisters and brothers of Jesus Christ and each other are we! Each of us, an image of *Abba*-God, is created, re-created, in Christ Jesus and called to develop our God-image. We are invited to live a fully human, a fully abundant, and a fully vibrant and vital life.

And each of us is born with the GIFT of two feeling and emotional capacities:
 1. the ability to *experience* feeling and emotion.
 2. the ability to *express* feeling and emotion.

Even in interuterine life, the fetus both experiences and expresses the state of being at-ease and in dis-ease, of being in comfort and in discomfort, of experiencing pleasure and annoyance, of displaying calmness and agitation. The four basic feelings and emotions of the infant can be readily discerned, even interpreted by an attentive adult: the baby can be *glad / sad / mad* (angry) / *scared* (fearful). Young infants are usually quite free in both experiencing and expressing their delight, their sadness, their annoyance, and their fears in and through their cries, their gurgling, their coos, and their smiles and screams.

These God-given human expressions of our feelings and emotions need to function freely and fully throughout the life span of each of us. These abilities are human energizers. They *do* provide the fuel for human movement and productive activity. A friend of mine got mileage from her anger fuel. Her "I'll-show-them" attitude propelled her through high school and college. Her eighth grade teacher had told her mother that Jane would never amount to much academically. Her mother concurred and then repeated the assessment to Jane. Whereupon, Jane resolved there and then that she would show them. The anger fuel worked well for Jane for over eight years. It was not until she was seriously involved with a young man and was engaged to be married, that she had to review her life and determine whether the approaching marriage would likewise be fueled with anger.

Feelings and emotions are central to our well-being as rational human beings. They provide us with the clues for our safety, for our protection, for our nurturance, for our intimacy with others. They can and do alert us both physiologically and psychologically to the impending pleasure and pain in our present situation. Cold hands, sweating palms, rapid breathing, increased pulse rate, a flushed face, and other bodily changes — all are clues to us and to others of the feeling and emotion we are experiencing. They are also central to establishing and maintaining satisfying relationships with others. They provide guidelines in reference to our intimacy/distance needs, our limitations, and our challenges in life. Again, they are central to our call to be and to become adult Christian women and men of the Gospel. The life and message of Jesus invites and summons the *whole* human person — mind, heart, spirit. The life and message of Jesus wants and welcomes a *total* response from each individual — mind, heart, spirit. In reality, feelings and emotions are to our adult Christian life what our five senses are to our human survival and well-being. They function as interior indicators of our personal security and insecurity in the presence of the reality of our present life situation. Our feelings and emotions provide us with a sense of our relationship with self, with our sisters and brothers in Christ, and with our *Abba*-God.

EXPERIENCING FEELING AND EMOTION

HUMAN EXPERIENCES of feeling and emotion are neither right nor wrong in themselves. The experience of a feeling or an emotion is an ethically neutral reality. Our experiences of feelings and emotions are our moments of self-truth. Contrary to the way many of us perceive our feeling and emotional experiences, there are no ethical or moral dimensions in merely experiencing feeling and emotion. To feel sad, annoyed, joyous, fearful, or resentful is only to exprience sadness, annoyance, joy, fear, or resentment. These experiences are valid and real for us. They can signal a clue, give a warning, sound a personal alert, convey a message which begs to be heard, to be heeded, and to be given due attention from us. For example, Patsy is participating in a parish planning meeting for the approaching annual parish fair. She listens to Roy, another parishioner who lives two blocks away, as he gives his report and his recommendations for the lighting needed for the fair site. Roy indicates that the designated area for booths housing the arts and crafts will not have as many floodlights as other places on the fairgrounds. The booth site will be darker than other places in the fair area. Patsy hears his recommendations and takes in the information. Almost imperceptibly, she becomes a bit restless, mildly agitated, somewhat uncomfortable. She begins fingering her ball-point pen and her feet start to wiggle within her sandles. She shifts and changes her body position. She straightens up, crosses her legs, and moves forward to lean more on the table in front of her. She clears her throat, tightens her hold on her pen, and quickly jots down a few words on the pad in front of her. "*Less light* in the booth area — a *dark* area! Address this!" What has happened here? Do we perceive discomfort? annoyance? delight? fear? sadness?

Patsy may or may not be aware that she is overtly expressing feeling and emotion. Her bodily movements are communicating that Roy's plans for the lighting of the fair site have "touched" her. Her level of conscious awareness of her feeling and emotion is still ambiguous, though. Her experiences are still neutral. They are neither good nor evil, neither right nor wrong, neither legal nor illegal. Yet her bodily movements are definitely communicating some message and signals about Patsy and her reaction to the darkness in the booth area of the fair. She is transmitting signals from her unconscious being, from her deepest self about what this darkness means to her. Patsy's body language is delivering a coded message which she and others need to hear and decipher. Her communication process is already functioning and sending out clues. *What* is Patsy experiencing? *How* is she feeling about the dark area? At some point during Roy's report, Patsy does consciously resolve to speak to the "dark area" issue. She chooses to express something of what she has been experiencing.

Many of us have serious questions about the validity of the ethical neutrality of our feeling and emotional experiences. For us to experience certain feelings and emotions is wrong, evil, even sinful. To feel sad, joyous, angry, or fearful is wrong. It is not lady-like. It is not manly. It is not Christian. Early in life many of us blocked out, put into our deep freeze, selected feelings and emotions. Certain feelings and emotional experiences were "No-No's!" for us. Perhaps important people in our early childhood censured us for expressing these feelings. These significant adults condemned, disapproved, ridiculed or even punished us when we expressed how we felt. The hidden messages of "Do not *feel* this! Do not *feel* that!" became our law, our rule, our commandment written in stone. We denied ourselves permission to feel certain things. These feelings were wrong and evil. So it is that many of us adults, especially we who are seeking adult Christian values and goals, have to *un-learn* and, then, *re-learn* full feeling and emotional experiences. Many women in our society have to melt the stone commandments, and resolve to give themselves their own permission to experience fully their anger and resentment. Many men in our society have to melt their stone commandments, and resolve to give themselves their own permission to experience fully their sadness and grief, their fear and anxiety.

Adult Christian living presupposes that human experiences of feeling and emotion are part and parcel of our daily living. The Good News of Jesus Christ demands multiple experiences of feeling and emotion from us in the diverse situations that shape our daily living. Day by day the Gospel summons us in personal freedom to rejoice in the Lord, to weep with those who are in sorrow and grief, and to be angry and indignant when we encounter others denying and negating the dignity and value of another human being.

The Gospel calls adults to participate in the prophetic mission of Jesus Christ. This prophetic role calls the Christian adult to comfort the afflicted, and to afflict the comfortable. This Gospel message invokes *free* and *full* human feeling and emotional experiences and awareness from us. We cannot participate in establishing the Kingdom of God without fully and freely experiencing feeling and emotion.

EXPRESSING FEELING AND EMOTION

OTHER PEOPLE, both in our past and in our present, have had and still do have a strong influence upon us in terms of our expression of feelings and emotions. The approval and disapproval of others (both past and present) become the laws, the norms, the demands, and the expectations which can determine our feeling and emotional expression and can influence our behavior. Influenced by others we have learned particular ways to express feeling and emotion, particular ways to suppress our expressions of feeling and emotion, and yes, even particular ways to mask our expressions of feeling and emotion.

In my home, my mother did the disciplining for ordinary misbehavior. Occasionally she spanked my sister; she found it necessary to spank me more often. I can clearly recall her injunction to me while spanking me one afternoon during the summer: "The more you cry, the more spanking you will get." It did not take me long to figure out how to minimize the amount of spanking I was to get. I chose to suppress any expression of pain, and definitely no expression of tears. Eventually, the day came when, after a vigorous spanking, I was able to stand up erect and triumphantly declare, "You did not hurt me at all!" Suppression and denial! Only years later did I discover my need to un-learn and then re-learn how to cry freely when I was experiencing hurt and sadness. I had to un-learn the denial and suppression of any expression of pain, and then to re-learn how to freely express my pain and sadness in a humane, adult manner.

Each of us chooses, makes decisions early in life about *how* we may express our feelings and emotions. We choose (influenced by others) how we are going to express joy, sadness, anger, frustration, jealously, fear, and anxiety. In the United States our choices about our expression of feeling and emotion tend to be related to sex differences — whether we are female or male. Our culture gives boys and men more permission to express with freedom their joy and gladness, their anger and resentment. More noise and physical movement is O.K. for the males in our society. "Boys will be boys!" Our culture gives girls and women more permission to express with freedom their sadness and grief, their fear and anxiety. Weeping, quasi-hysterical agitation, and moaning and sighing are O.K. for the female. "Girls need to do that!" Women are not supposed (permission denied) to laugh boisterously or to express strong verbal and physical anger. "Be lady-like! Please others!" Men are not supposed (permission denied) to express freely their hurt and sadness by weeping openly or publicly. "Be manly! Please others!"

We cannot consistently block, suppress, and mask our feelings and emotions without serious harm to our living with and in the truth of our own personhood. We can harm our relationship with ourselves, and we can seriously endanger our relationships with others. Genuine intimacy cannot exist in relationships that lack full feeling and emotional experiences, nor can it exist in relationships that lack free expression and sharing of feeling and emotion. Many men express anger when they are in reality experiencing hurt, sadness, or fear. This is bizarre behavior insofar as the expression does not reflect their real feeling and emotional experience. Their outward expression lacks the truth and the validity of their inner experience. Such bizarre behavior indicates that we are not revealing the truth of our feeling and emotional experiences. Many women in our culture also behave bizarrely when communicating and expressing their feelings and emotions. Many women weep and lament when in reality they are experiencing anger, annoyance, and indignation. My own statement in response to the spanking, "You did not hurt me at all!" was a lie, an untruth. Physically and psychologically I was in pain. I was hurting. My expression was an angry, defiant communication, yet it did not honestly convey what I was experiencing during the spanking. I suppressed and denied my inner truth. Yes, it hurt, and I was hurting. As adults we need to review and reflect upon the truth and the reality of our expressions of feeling and emotion. Our self-truth needs to be released, shared, and given to others in an adult, humane manner. When we lock in, block off, and dam up our genuine feelings and emotions, no wonder there are strange and bizarre volcanic reactions with others at unexpected and inappropriate times and places. Bizarre behavior is a function of past untruthful, dishonest expressions of feelings and emotions. We live the lie; we express the lie to self and to others.

Obviously, there is an ethic, a morality connected with our expression of feelings and emotions. There are right and wrong, appropriate and inappropriate, good and evil, legal and illegal "how to's" which govern adult, humane expressions of feeling and emotion. *Experiencing* feeling and emotion is one type of human affective behavior. *Expressing* our feeling and emotion is another and different kind of human affective behavior. Our expressions of feeling and emotion *do* possess ethical and moral norms and consequences. Each of us has to, at some point in our adult life, reassess both the freedom and the truth of our adult expressions of feeling and emotion.

We are not born with our cultural norms and laws ingrained in our behavioral repertoire. We have to learn how to express our feelings and emotions in a free, adult manner. Inordinate tendencies in our communication of feeling and emotion need to be tamed and checked. On the other hand, we need to be freed from false suppression and unhealthy masking of our genuine feelings and emotions. Free and full adulthood demands this homework from us.

Free and full feeling and emotional behavior leads, brings, and draws us into adult Christian living. We can enjoy both *being* the truth in love and also *doing* the truth in love. We can possess Gospel transparency. Insofar as there exists a high correlation between our experience and expression of feeling and emotion, we can participate in Gospel transparency. Our spirit has a crystal-like quality to it. Genuine communication and realistic community experiences are possible for us. Genuine dialogue, rather than evasive sterile monologue, becomes possible to us in our adult encounters and interactions with others.

Mature, adult Christian living is diluted and weakened without mature and honest affective behavior. Free and full Gospel rejoicing, free and full Gospel praising, free and full Gospel thanksgiving, free and full Gospel sorrowing, free and full Gospel fearing, free and full Gospel compassion, free and full Gospel groaning cannot be ours without free and full feeling and emotional behavior. Each of us is human, yet the Gospel invites each of us to become humane. There is much un-learning and re-learning that we are called to do in order for the human person within us to be actualized and become humane. Our call to change, our call to conversion, is the adult renewal which Christ Jesus asks of us. And feelings and emotions are inextricably involved in the call to be converted, to change, to repent, to be renewed.

ADULT RESPONSIBILITY AND FEELING AND EMOTIONAL BEHAVIOR

EACH OF US is responsible for how we handle the experiences and the expressions of our feeling and emotional life. No one else can assume this responsibility for us. Our taking hold of our responsibility determines the line of demarcation between adult and pre-adult behavior. As adults, we can and do choose to be glad, sad, mad (angry), and scared (fearful). Personal choice and decision are significant in terms of mature affective behavior. Each of us chooses *what* we will feel, and *how* we will express and share our feelings and emotions with others. Other people *do not make* us glad, sad, mad, and scared, *unless* we ourselves give them the power to do so. We allow them; we let them; and at times we even demand that they make us glad, sad, mad, or scared. We empower other people. *We* give others power over us, over our feeling and emotional experiences and expressions. We choose to be their victims; we choose to have others regulate our moods, our powers, and the feeling focus of our affective energy. *We* surrender and give up our own feeling and emotional responsibility and decision-making power to others. Our surrender indicates that we consider moods, the affective power, and human energies of others more valuable and dependable than our own. Ours are worthless, ours are not reliable, and so we do not trust our own feelings and emotions. Others give us direction and movement. We abdicate the driver's seat behind the wheel of our personhood, and we are more content and secure seated in the front passenger seat. Perhaps, some of us even consign ourselves to the back seat! There, as self-displaced drivers, we can and do agitate the self-substituted driver with our aggressive questions and anxieties.

In terms of our feeling and emotional behavior, we choose the passenger or back-seat driver pattern and life style.

We release to others the power to tell us how we should feel — "You shouldn't feel that way!" The tragedy of this situation is that we abandon both our GIFT and our human right to function with personal conviction and commitment. Emotionally, we soon become parasites drawing our energy from other people's energy. We refuse to generate and utilize our own God-given feeling and emotional energies. We merely exist. And we live symbiotically in terms of our affective experiences and expressions and communication. When we love another person, we release to the loved one certain powers with and over us. And feeling and emotional experiences accompany our decision to love. In loving ourselves, we entrust ourselves with the responsibility for our own protection and nurturance. When we love another, we share our self-entrusted selves with the other. We still retain, however, the responsibility to protect and to nurture ourselves, even though we share our love with another. To choose to love another does not mean that we assume the responsibility to protect and to nurture her/him. Choosing to love another person means that as adults we assume that our loved one is already fulfilling her/his adult task of self-nurturance and self-protection. Only children have the right to expect nurturance and protection from adults. Loving children is different. When we assume the parenting role, we do intend to nurture and to protect our children. The younger they are, the more they need our parenting care.

Abba-God has created each of us as a beautiful luxury car. This is an image of ourselves with which we can readily identify. We are completely and efficiently equipped. Power steering, power brakes, multi-cylinder engine power, cruise control, and beauty of line and design are all ours; the ignition of our car is ready to start up under our direction and control. Some of us even deny that we are a luxury car. We resist registering our car in our own name. We have an additional God-given task of maintaining our tires. We and only we are supposed to inflate the tires of our vehicle. However, we resist doing our job of maintaining the tires. We prefer others to inflate them and we ignore our obligation. Some of us can and have spent years immobile and stranded on a section of our life road demanding that friends and passersby fix and inflate our flat tires. We are not aware that when others take over our job with our tires, they are able to sabotage our movement by deflating our tires. How comical we are! Ultimately, only we can inflate our tires effectively.

ABBA-GOD AND FEELINGS AND EMOTIONS

Abba-GOD, the God of Jesus Christ, reveals in the Scriptures — both Hebrew and Christian — strong feeling and emotion. The God of the Scriptures is not the God of the philosophers — distanced from us, impersonal, objective, and removed from our human situation. The Scriptures present and reveal our God to be deeply, radically involved with his people. Jesus, our Emmanuel, God-with-us, came to dwell among us, came and pitched his tent among us. The Spirit is sent to be with us. The Scriptures reveal our God to be a God who acts. Our *Abba*-God in his dealings with us is compassionate, forgiving, loving, encouraging, healing, embracing, comforting, challenging, and protecting. All of these actions and initiatives have profoundly intense and deep emotional meaning for us. We can recall several of these:

Because you are precious in my eyes and glorious,
> and because I love you... (Is 43:4).

Fear not, O Jacob, my servant,
> the darling whom I have chosen,
I will pour out water upon the thirsty ground,
> and streams upon the dry land;
I will pour out my spirit upon your offspring,
> and my blessing upon your descendants (Is 44:3).

Rejoice with me because I have found my lost sheep (Lk 15:6).

The Lord saw this (evil) and was aggrieved
> that right did not exist.
He saw that there was no one,
> and was appalled that there was none to intervene;
So his own arm brought about the victory,
> and his justice lent him its support (Is 60:16).

He (Jesus) looked around at them with anger,
> for he was deeply grieved
that they had closed their minds against him (Mk 3:5).

Abba-God, the God of Jesus Christ, the God of the Scriptures (Hebrew and Christian) is a God of action, initiative and outreach. In Christ Jesus we are called to decision, to choice, and to action in terms of our feeling and emotional behavior. Truly we can pray with the Psalmist, "I give you thanks that I am fearfully, wonderfully made" (Ps 139:14).

SUMMARY

OUR HUMAN FEELINGS AND EMOTIONS are central to our adult, human behavior. Joy and life-delight, sadness and hurt, anger and resentment, fear and anxiety — these feelings and emotions weave and design the fabric of our personal and social relationships. Also, our religious experiences resonate with the power and energy of this inner affective awareness.

Each of us is born with the GIFT of twofold feeling and emotional capacities:

1. The ability to *experience* feeling and emotion.
2. The ability to *express* feeling and emotion.

The Good News of Jesus Christ invites and summons the *whole* human person — mind, heart, spirit. Adult Christian living activates and calls forth both our feeling and emotional experience and expression.

Our experiences of feeling and emotion are ethically neutral. These experiences are signals. They call us to listen to them, to attend to them, and to reflect upon their significance and meaning. Inner subjective realities need to emerge from within our consciousness and need to be interpreted in the light of their value in our life. Many of us deny, ignore, and even freeze these calls for reflection. The Gospel message of Jesus insists that we keep in close and intimate relationship with our feelings and emotional experiences.

Our expression of feeling and emotion has ethical and moral consequences. We possess numerous options and choices which determine *how* we express our feelings and emotions. When we are angry we can choose to remain silent, speak about the anger, deny the anger and pretend to be calm, verbally abuse another, physically attack the other or proceed to tear up the furnishings of a room. Our early childhood influenced each of us in relation to our expressions of feelings and emotions. As adults, we have eliminated some earlier options and have chosen to express our feelings and emotions in selected and particular ways. Adulthood is the time to review and to reconsider the multiple options open to us in our expression of feeling and emotion. Adulthood is our "re-negotiation time" in terms of our affective expressions. Earlier options that were dismissed as either inappropriate or impossible for us can now be chosen with freedom. Earlier options that were chosen may need to be negated, so that other and more mature options can be part of our behavior. As adults, we can and do need to un-learn, and then re-learn ways of expressing our feelings and emotions. Learning is a continual process for mature adults.

Each of us is responsible for the movement and challenge that continual learning asks of us. Others do not make us glad, sad, mad, and scared. We give and surrender to them the power to impose their feelings and emotions upon us. When we love another person, we release to our loved one some power over us. Feeling and emotional experiences do accompany our decisions to love. In loving ourselves, we entrust ourself to ourself to protect and to nurture. When we love another, we share our self-entrusted self with another. And yet, we still hold the responsibility to protect and to nurture ourselves, even though we share our love with our loved one.

Abba-God, our Parenting God, nurtures and protects our spirit life. Comforting and confronting are significant initiatives in his active loving-kindness towards us. Our God of the Scriptures is involved with us, and participates in our life with an active, continual presence. The God of Jesus Christ reveals compassion, forgiveness, encouragement, healing, and challenge to us. Our experiences and expressions of feeling and emotion are vital to a mature response to ourselves, to others, and to our *Abba*-God.

TWO

Gladness, Life-Delight, Joy, And Pleasure

INTRODUCTION

HUMAN MATURITY is a quality that we all wish to have, to possess, and to be able to call forth at will. What is the usual meaning of maturity? Maturity is our capacity, our ability, to generate, to produce, or to discover new realities within our lives. Maturity is not so much an end point in human life as it is an index of our consistent and continual growth and development. Human maturity addresses many areas of our life. It is a life-long process. There are many different dimensions to our maturation. Sexually, we are mature when we can reproduce the species. Intellectually, we are mature when we are able to produce an original thought, idea, or insight. We discover new meaning for ourselves (the a-ha! experience). There are adults who are well educated who do not generate their own thoughts and insights, but are rather content to parrot the ideas and opinions of others. Emotionally, we are mature when we can and do produce positive feelings regarding self and others. We are self-activating emotionally, and we do not depend upon others to make us happy, to make us feel good about ourselves. Spiritually, we are mature when we can and do protect and nurture our gifts of the spirit — peace, joy, patience in our life situation. We welcome and cherish the peace and joy of Christ.

Each of us is responsible for generating and producing an atmosphere of good feeling and a positive emotional climate for herself/himself and for others. We choose. We decide. Whether others choose to accept and to interact with our sharing is another issue. Nevertheless, our emotional maturity depends upon our choices and decisions. We opt for the positive or the negative.

OUR CAPACITY FOR JOY

ASHLEY MONTAGU insists that the child is naturally inclined to joy, and has an inborn capacity for it. He maintains that in our Western world there has been a "massive failure" on our part to recognize the importance of joy as a developmental need and a vital necessity for living. "Parents, teachers, coaches and spectators all seem to be engaged in a conspiracy to take the joy out of games" (*Growing Young*, p. 177). He considers that playing for fun and for pleasure is a lost art for us Westerners. And we are the losers.

How do we experience the gladness, the delight, and the joy of life? How do we bring about these feelings in our lives? Whenever we personally experience joy and pleasure in life we become aware of ourselves as enhanced and enriched. A sense of vitality, vigor, and well-being pervades our self-awareness. These feelings can be reassuring and delightful. The pleasure of these experiences energizes and empowers us. We celebrate being alive and being in relationship with others. Our being sings! Our music may be expressed by the simplicity of a flute solo, or it may require the depth and breadth of a large orchestra soaring in unity and harmony to a crescendo in a full-scale symphony. The musical expression works. The sound resonates with clarity of expression, fullness of participation, firm direction and control. Our experiences of being well, working well, and relating well with others are part of what our pleasure and delight in life are all about. Our past decisions and choices have brought us into these experiences of fullness and joy. Moreover our past decisions and choices may have brought us into our present misery, our present negativism, our present boredom and listlessness. As in all experiences of feeling and emotion, there are varying depths to our awareness. These levels of feeling and emotional experiences within us are like the graduated depths of a large swimming pool. The various levels — one foot, three feet, five feet, seven feet, nine feet — engage us in multiple ways. Certainly a one-foot anger experience (simple annoyance) evokes a qualitatively different expression from that of a nine-foot anger experience. Yet, it is essential that we be in the pool, experiencing and expressing our life situation realistically, rather than separated and alienated from our feelings and emotions. Staying pool-side is opting for denial, withdrawal from self and others, and immaturity. Maturity in terms of our emotional behavior provides us with the assurance that our decisions and choices include opportunities for gladness, life-delight, pleasure and joy. We ourselves have to choose the diet which adequately feeds, nourishes, and strengthens our experiences and expressions of life-delight and joy.

STRATEGIES FOR JOY

M. SCOTT PECK, in his *The Road Less Traveled*, offers selected strategies for taking hold of and acting responsibly in terms of choosing to experience joy and delight in our daily living. Many people have found these suggestions to be helpful and life-giving. His recommendations are these:

1. *Choose to provide for yourself sufficient physical sensory stimulation.* Our five senses, taste, touch, hearing, smell, and sight afford us innumerable opportunities for pleasure and joy. Our God-given sensuality is intended to function as a source of personal pleasure and enjoyment. Let us reflect upon these reservoirs of life-delight.

Taste provides us with daily chances to enjoy and take delight in our need for nourishment. Taking the time and making the effort to savor our selected food and drink is an exercise in sensitivity and refinement. Especially here in the United States, where there are so many food options and choices, there is little excuse for meals to be dull, tasteless, and routine. True, because our busy schedules can tempt us into frequently "grabbing a bite to eat" and "eating on the run," we do need to stop from time to time and review our eating habits. Animals eat; humans dine. We choose to share our time and presence with others during a meal. Any meal can have a sacred meaning. Inherent in any meal is a death-life issue. The fruits of the field, the animals of the land, and the fish of the sea die, surrender their lives, so that they may live again, come to life again within us. Life is given for life. All food is the fruit of the labor of many people in addition to being the life-gift of plant, animal, and fish. Furthermore, sharing a meal with others calls us to attend both to the meal and to the presence of others at our table. We are nourished both individually and socially when we dine. Merely to eat, to gulp down food, in order to satisfy hunger pangs is not a human action. Rather, it is bestial. Recently, several hotels in New Orleans have offered the public English high tea daily in the afternoon. The menu consists of a choice of international teas, finger sandwiches, hot scones with assorted jams, cream, butter, and cookies (biscuits) and sweets. The ambiance is leisurely, relaxed and laid back. Groups gather around a low table conversing and savoring the three courses. Chamber music is playing. The entire scene contrasts strongly with the rushed, noisy, and harsh surroundings of many restaurants and fast-food eateries. It provides a leisurely, gentle, nurturing experience.

Touch is another pleasurable sensory experience. The feel of sun, wind, and water upon us can be a delightful sensation. Children love to hug and to hold their worn stuffed animals, dragged-all-over-the-place pillows, and raggedy old blankets. Leo Buscaglia recommends frequent hugs each day for the affirmation and reassurance that they give to us. Even medical schools and centers are recommending that medical personnel touch their patients more. A pat on the back, a handshake, stroking another's arm — all give signals of caring, humaneness, and a compassionate attitude towards others. Ma Bell's slogan, "Reach Out and Touch Someone" has surfaced an important issue in our culture. It focusses in upon a responsive chord in our distanced, touch-me-not society. Many of us adults are touch-deprived in our sophisticated culture.

One day in the early evening just before our meal, I met one of our older retired sisters who had a special sparkle in her eyes. I knew she had been into something important to her that day. When I asked her about her "glow," she told me how wonderful her afternoon was. Anytime she was free for a few hours, she would take the local bus over to St. Vincent's Infant Home. Once there, she would go directly to the nursery, pick up the infants, hold them to her, and then sing to them. Beaming with joy and delight she said, "They need being sung to and skin-on-skin care." Currently, psychologists are addressing the need for stroking that each of us has. This stroking need is not only verbal in terms of praise and affirmation, but the need is also physical.

Hearing can be another source of human pleasure and delight. Sounds for us can be soothing, joyful, frightening, and stimulating. People's voices, traffic noises, mechanical sounds, nature's messages, music — all contribute daily to our auditory repertoire. Yes, we speak of "turning people off" and "tuning them out," yet what sounds and messages of pleasure do we choose to "turn on" to or "tune into"? What sounds do we choose to allow to flow into us, into our being?

Smell is another marvelous resource for human pleasure. Kitchen odors — baking, frying, broiling, and simmering of foods — can be a delight. Nature and creation also release some very pleasurable odors — trees, vines, flowers, lakes, rivers, and oceans — each has its own pleasant sensual scents. Humanists are ever encouraging us "to stop and smell the roses." Odors, as we know, are specific to particular persons, places, and things. The one remaining streetcar line in New Orleans has its own odor. I didn't realize this until I had been out of the city for over six years, even though I grew up in New Orleans. One humid September morning, I was waiting for the St. Charles streetcar. As it lumbered toward me, I was inundated with that peculiar electric-motor-wheel-on-steel-track smell. A warm reverie immediately enfolded me — high school days to and from school, years of climbing aboard and tumbling out as the streetcar screeched to a halt. That odor, evoking memories recapturing the familiar past and linking it to my present, was precious to me. It alerted me that I was on home turf, with its unique home-town smell.

Sight is another sensory avenue which can provide us with multiple opportunities for sensory joy and pleasure. How many of us have had someone exclaim with joy, "You are a sight for sore eyes!" Many of us with more than adequate vision seldom really see what is in our line of vision. Vacant stares and the surface-scanning of people, places, and events characterize much of our sight-seeing. Without personal time, attention, and focus we do not really see, take in the beauty and power within nature, within technology, and especially within the people around us. Some of us function like an empty, filmless camera. We cavort about clicking away, yet are never really impressed or imprinted by the beauty and significance of what we see. The world of creation and nature beckons to us, and people also invite us to see them in all their beauty and uniqueness. Each reality provides us with an occasion to celebrate its being, its vitality, its singular purpose and function. Yet, bias, prejudice, and so much personal blindness negate the possibility of our experiencing joy and delight in the vision of the remarkable other. At times, we need to step back and distance ourselves from the people with whom we live and work, so that we can see them in a fresh, new, and original light.

The Scriptures are filled with accounts of sensory experiences and expressions. All five senses are mentioned in reference to our response to Christ Jesus and his message. "Taste and see." We hear the Word. "He (Jesus) reached out his hand and touched her." "You have eyes and do not see." We walk in the sweet odor of Christ. God's presence in sights, sounds, smells, touch, and taste needs to be explored and enjoyed. Theologians are aware of this and are concerned about the technological emphasis of our Western culture hardening our sensibilities. We can become too much like the steel, the plastic, and the concrete which are becoming the hallmarks of our culture. Urban dwellers do need more time with and in nature to regain their humaneness. Our experiences can become one-sided, with too much emphasis upon science and technology. Edward Schillebeeckx deplores this when he writes:

"As a result of this one-sidedness, modern Western man has become alienated from the sphere of his original experiences. Our capacity to see and hear, to taste and to smell, our perception and our spirit . . . have been blunted by the one-sided uses of science and technology" (*Christ*, p. 805).

2. *Choose to provide for yourself opportunities for discovery.* The exploratory process is part of our human personhood. We can observe our young, in their delight and pleasure when investigating and struggling to discover, to learn something new. It begins to wane and to weaken when immature and impatient adults discourage and at times castigate them for their God-given and God-pulsating curiosity. Little wonder that Peggy Lee's *Is That All There Is?* was such a hit across the nation. We allow ourselves to be buried within the cement of our routine, our same old meaningless rituals. We choose merely to go through the motions of our lives, oblivious of meaning and then spend so much time and energy whining about how dull, how boring and how uneventful our lives are. We have not been created to function as machines do — with precision, leaving no room for deviation or margin for change. We are created to explore, to discover the new, to find the surprises in our life stream.

I have always been amused by the relationship of the exclamation point (!) to the question mark (?). Without question marks in our life, there are few, maybe no exclamation points. An exclamation point is the response to a question, a question mark which has been taken seriously by us. When we choose to explore life, to entertain questions seriously, we bring into our world another dimension of human life — meaning. Our human spirit thirsts more for meaning than it does for information. Through our active involvement in exploring, questing or questioning, and investigating the unknown and the possible, we create possibilities of joy and delight for ourselves. Otherwise, we decline and descend into mere passive, somnolent, and anesthetized living.

New experiences and awarenesses serve to stimulate and to arouse the reflective processes within us. Moving in and with the flow of the new carries us into insights and relationships that are their own reward. The Christian liturgy frequently invites us to "Sing a NEW song to the Lord!" For many of us, this is an impossibility. The Gospel calls us both continually and consistently to reform, reshape, renew our lives. This is a call to newness, to discover the newness of change, of move- ment, and of challenge. This call endeavors to counteract the sloth, the laziness, and the resistance to change within each of us.

3. *Choose to provide for yourself opportunities for mastery and achievement.* Exploring the new is not sufficient for intelligent, questioning, mature adults. Consciously and conscientiously mastering new and different ventures is important for our personal development. Frequently, we need to taste the "I-did-it!" experience. We can take pride in confronting both the expected and the unexpected, and then carrying them off adequately, even well. Successful completion of our work brings its own joy and satisfaction. Innumerable options for a sense of mastery exist in our lives. Taking hold of our daily responsibilities, the tasks and jobs that must be done as well as the new opportunities that we encounter, provides us with many mastery opportunities. Many of us do not give ourselves sufficient praise and affirmation for the multiple things we accomplish each day which demand attention, energy, and time from us. We tend to take ourselves for granted (granite!) in these attention-demanding, time-demanding jobs. Taking pride in our usual day-by-day achievements and accomplishments can increase the sense of joy and pleasure in our lives. We need the daily self-recognition and self-ownership of handling well our day's challenges and duties. Mastering the mundane can be monumental for us. Many of us ignore, even deny, the excellence and industry we bring to the ordinary duties of our day. Meal preparation, providing for and clothing our children, our home management, and the

maintenance of our appliances and cars, our career nitty-gritty, meeting the deadlines that confront us each week, each month — all of these require tremendous attention, focus, discipline, and courage from us. We need to name and to claim these doings and activities. We are into mastery, and we are handling well many significant jobs within our life. In managing our life at home and within our professional and work environments, we are achieving much more than we give ourselves credit for. Truth demands that we recognize and acknowledge the daily mastery of the events of our lives. Many of us in addition to these usual tasks, also take on new challenges to conquer. Hobbies, volunteer work and participation in social groups give us numerous other chances for mastering new skills, new relationships, new challenges.

4. *Choose to provide creative experiences for yourself.* Most of us are more creative than we are willing to admit. We frequently deny that we are creative people. Creative problem solving is part of our practical and inventive American way of life. Our drugstores and bookstores have shelves filled with how-to literature. The variety of uses to which we put plastic sheets, aluminum foil, and plywood is astounding. Re-creating, renovating, refurbishing are an ongoing process in many of our homes and neighborhoods. We create our own quilting designs, our own recipes, our own audio-sound systems, our own patios and decks, our own mix-and-match wardrobes, our own model trains and miniature towns, our own home decoration and landscaping, and the list could go on and on. And yet, some of us need to survey our own lifestyles and situations in terms of our creative experiences and expressions. Where in my life is creativity — making and doing something new and different — functioning well *now*? At this time in our lives, how are we choosing to function creatively? How are we working with options, goals, and purposes in creating our future?

Much of our creativity comes to the fore when we are goal oriented, and when we live with purpose and meaning. Some of us merely float; we allow ourself to be drawn by the current of other people's purposes and goals rather than establish our own goals or actively participate in mutually agreed upon goals and direction. When we establish our own goals and direction, we are usually willing, even eager, to expend energy and time in achieving those goals. We endure and even learn from temporary setbacks, as we creatively confront and assess them. So it is that we humbly co-create our future with *Abba*-God and others. We take responsibility for our God-given life and destiny.

5. *Choose to provide opportunities for your immersion into projects and endeavors.* For some of us our career involvement is self-consuming. We generously plunge ourselves into our work, investing it with all our energy and genuine interest. For us it is easy to let go and lose our sense of self and our awareness of time in our work. We invest. And yet, for others, work is merely putting in the necessary time. There is little personal interest and commitment. Working is only earning a living — nothing more, nothing less. Our hobbies and our family claim our interest and our personal investment. These personal commitments make our life worthwhile. We lose ourselves in these activities.

Hobbies such as hunting, fishing, reading, playing and listening to music, sports, mechanics, cooking, sewing, dancing, carpentry — each of these and many others provide opportunities for getting caught up in interesting leisure-time activities which expand and renew our human spirit. They fill and feed our spirit. We enjoy them. They protect us from too much harsh, draining and demanding reality. They make us feel better about ourselves and enable us to relate to others in a more humane manner, especially when we "do our own thing" periodically and consistently. Our hobbies break into our daily duties and take hold of us. They distance us from our daily "have to"s, "must"s, and "should"s. They gift us with temporary respite and refreshment.

Hobbies and personal projects give us play time, enjoying-life time, pleasure time. When we invest ourself in hobbies, we give ourself permission to enjoy and relish our lives, and to take pleasure in our adult interests. We are not machines. We cannot for long periods of time switch on to automatic pilot and fly above our legitimate human need for pleasure and joy. We have to turn off our engine, come down to reality, and touch base with our human needs. The earth-child within each of us needs to enjoy, to play, and to take delight in the roots of our being/doing humanity. Each of us truly needs wings and roots. Our wings carry us to numerous personal and social obligations and duties, many of which bring us joy and delight. On the other hand our roots give us a sense of permanence, simplicity and genuine earthiness in terms of our capacity for enjoyment, pleasure, and life-delight.

6. *Choose to provide for yourself opportunities for becoming one with others.* We can expand our horizons and grow as individuals when we participate in activities which are social. Identifying with a larger group can bring its own enrichment and sense of vigor and vitality. The nineteenth century Roman Catholic immigrants to the Protestant United States experienced this sense of enlarged identity with the Roman Catholic Church when they left their homeland and came to the new world. The universal Church was important to them and to their identity. In leaving their homeland and their national identity, they were vulnerable and helpless. Their parish church was far more than a local reality for them; it symbolized the all-over-the-world Church. They belonged to a powerful, world-wide, universal (yes, holy) reality — the Roman Catholic Church. In a very real way, these immigrant

people needed the local church, the local parish. We need to recall that they were without status, without jobs, without adequate formal education, and without citizenship.

Yes, each of us has needs to belong. Implicit within our personal identity is a sense of belonging. Each of us has to enjoy some solid, social affirmation of our individual personhood. Erik Erikson (*Identity*) indicates that individual identity is achieved in and through social affirmation. Each of us lives within a specific and unique social context. Our fusion, our belonging with others, our social affirmation are important for mature adult living. For each of us, there are social affiliations that characterize our identity. For instance, I am an Irish American; I name and claim this. I am from the deep South; I name and claim this. I am Roman Catholic; I name and claim this. I am a Dominican woman religious; I name and claim this. I am female; I name and claim this. I am a human person; I name and claim this. Each naming and claiming asserts with whom my specific life and life experiences are associated.

In addition to these broad identifications, I also enjoy other people and groups with whom I enjoy mutuality in sharing interests, values, and concerns. Most of us need to be part of a larger social group. We need to identify and to participate with other meaningful groups which affirm both our individual experiences and expressions of life interests and values. Church groups, support groups, prayer groups, garden clubs, political organizations, school groups, discussion groups — all can contribute to enlarging our lifestyle and life awareness. For adult Christians, this experience of belonging is very significant. We belong to *Abba*-God. We belong to Jesus, our Brother and our Savior. We belong to each other in the Spirit; we are sisters and brothers. St. Peter's message roots us in our Gospel affiliations:

You, however, are a chosen race,
a royal priesthood,
a holy nation,
a people he claims for his own
to proclaim the glorious works of the One who called
you from darkness into his marvelous light (1 P 2:9).

7. *Choose to provide for yourself opportunities for transcendent experiences.* Each of us knows times when we have had an unusual, significant, peak experience. We cannot and will not ever forget it. It touched us. It seared itself indelibly within our being. Somehow, we emerged a bit different from the experience. These individual special events, these high energy and deeply perceptive moments can nurture and feed us for a long period of time. Even if we do not penetrate their meaning and significance, even if we do not understand them fully, they nourish us. Within our peak experiences, we are aware of ourselves as part of and united with all of reality; these experiences are universal and cosmic experiences. They enable us to transcend our individual and specific social and group identifications. They go beyond our usual life experiences. They grasp us. They lift us up, beyond and away from our concrete personal awarenesses. We are one with the whole world, the cosmos, yes even with our *Abba*-God. This experience is an *I AM* experience; *I AM* everyone, everything, everywhere. We are all one and our experience validates this reality.

Many of us become fearful when we are blessed with a transcendent experience. We are afraid of the consequences: Are we going crazy? Dare we share this with anyone? What will other people think? We need to relax with and enjoy the loveliness of our experience. Some of us panic when this surprise awareness invades and enters our ordinary mundane consciousness. Our lives are a struggle with the milk and honey of daily living. The milk (survival, substance, unusual duties) engages us day after day; the honey (joy, delight, the unexpected surprise) is sheer gift which breaks into and enhances our normal routine.

These seven strategies call us out of our deadening routine, our inner sloth, and our personal apathy. Each strategy insists upon personal choice and decision regarding a life style which can include joy, gladness, and pleasure. We can become both responsible for and accountable to ourselves for the movement and energy within our daily lives. The Good News of Jesus Christ invites each of us to experience the vitality, the abundance, the vigor of adult humane living. Our own choices and decisions can and do determine the personal delight, pleasure, and joy within our present life experiences.

Our expression of personal joy and delight reaches out expansively to self, to others, and to our *Abba*-God. Both our individual and social activities radiate our joy and gladness. Our feelings and emotional experiences of joy and delight enlarge our personal vistas, enhance our awareness of self, and energize us to reach out in joy to others. With others in our family, in our work, and in our recreation, we can radiate peace, joy, and patience. We are Gospel people of breadth and depth; we are Gospel people of praise and thanksgiving. We are actively adult in our Gospel living and sharing. We carry within us and to others the Good News in our ordinary and concrete daily doings and involvements. The gift of joy and delight that we have received is freely shared with and extended to others. Our mature joy and gladness serves to generate within others joy and life-delight. We become adult Gospel bearers, not merely in speech, but in the fullness of our being, our spirit. With Mary we can sing our Magnificat, "My soul (my spirit, my being) proclaims the greatness of the Lord, and my spirit rejoices in God my Savior!" (Lk 1:46).

SUMMARY

OUR MATURITY involves our ability to produce, to generate, and to discover pleasure and joy within our own life. Each of us enjoys the responsibility to make decisions and choices which can produce and generate gladness, life-delight, pleasure, and joy in our life. Yet, our own inner sloth and laziness militate against our mature and full adult emotional living. We cannot expect or demand that others make us happy, bring us joy, and provide pleasurable experiences for us. Not to assume our responsibility for life-delight is to surrender ourself to negativism and resentment by personal default. Then we can indulge ourselves in choosing to feel dull, bored, trapped, helpless, and hopeless. By default we freely decide to submit to and to experience these negative feelings.

M. Scott Peck, in his *The Road Less Traveled*, suggests seven ways of creating our future with an anticipation of experiencing personal joy, life-delight, and pleasure. His recommendations are these:

1. Choose sufficient physical, sensory stimulation.
2. Choose to provide opportunities for personal discovery in our lives.
3. Choose to provide opportunities for mastery and achievement in our lives.
4. Choose to provide creative experiences for ourselves.
5. Choose to immerse ourselves in projects, individual interests, and hobbies.
6. Choose opportunities for joining with others in social activities.
7. Choose opportunities for transcendent experiences to emerge from within our lives.

Each of these seven options for mature and adult living requires personal reflection, personal time, and personal energy and commitment from us. Without personal commitment to life, in all its fullness, we let go of and surrender our personal power to fashion our future. We then choose victimhood as a lifestyle. The Gospel summons us to participate fully in our life, in our future. Our active involvement brings both direction and purpose into the ebb and flow of our lives. We deserve to enjoy life, to engage life in its fullness, and to taste the delight of life. Mature, adult decisions and choices usher us into the pleasure and gladness of life. We then become women and men of the Gospel; we become women and men of Gospel-praise and Gospel-thanksgiving. The decisions and choices are ours!

THREE

Sadness And Grief, Mourning And Loss

INTRODUCTION

SAYING "Good-Bye" and moving on can be painful and uncomfortable. I experience the pain of departure frequently in my travelling. Getting settled in a hotel room or the guest quarters of a conference or retreat center is a temporary rooting for me. Each time I unpack completely; getting my clothing, books, notes and toilet articles in place is part of my initial settling-in routine. Then, on to meeting new people, interacting and sharing with the group, spending some personal time and energy with specific folks — all are investing functions of any guest speaker. And yet, my room or guest quarters is my base, my temporary haven away from home. Soon enough, my work is completed. Finally it is time to leave, to move on. Packing up, bidding farewell to my hosts and new friends and the particular space I have occupied always brings to me some experience of sadness. Scanning the room to be sure that I have left nothing behind, I occasionally whisper, "Goodbye, little room!" I die a little each time I settle in and then have to leave a place.

Our human life is an active process. It is a life-long experience of much movement and frequent change, and it encompasses new, unfamiliar encounters and interactions with other people. New emerging processes are in motion — strangers becoming known, acquaintances becoming friends. New developments emerge within our life, our family, and our career situations. People enter into our lives, change and modify them along with our attitudes and our vision of life. People also leave our life scene through death, distance in space and time, diversity in interests and lifestyle. We experience separation and loss. An essential dimension of adult living is letting go and moving on. Our life journey invites us to meet, greet, and then bid farewell to numerous people along the way.

Sadness is our experience of grief, mourning, and loss which accompanies our letting go, bidding farewell, and having to move on. Our past experiences and relationships represent the investment we have made of ourselves, our time, energy, interest and concern that we've shared with people, in places that have become significant as we took part in things that enriched and increased the value of both our experiences and our relationships. Sadness is a divesting feeling and emotional experience. We divest ourselves or are divested of sharing time, places, and personal involvement with others who are important in our lives. We feel like a radically pruned rose bush, unable to reach out, unable to catch the wind, unable to enjoy the perfume of our blossoming and flowering. We cut off, and we are cut off from, habitual ways of being and doing with others, especially a familiar loved one.

OUR EXPERIENCE OF
DEATH — SADNESS AND GRIEF

THE DEATH OF A LOVED ONE — a parent, a spouse, a child, a sister, a brother, a close friend — is a dramatic example of the experience of sadness, grief, mourning, and loss. We are called to let go. In our spatial and temporal awareness we are separated, cut off from our familiar, cherished manner of relating to our loved one. We cannot in our usual way visit together, share a meal together, enjoy television and movies together, exchange viewpoints about the issues of our life situation. We experience a void, a vacuum, an emptiness in our personal and social life that is deeply personal. Some part of ourselves has gone with the departed persons; something of us has also died. Our experience of this personal loss is painful, even agonizing. We hurt. We grieve and mourn. We are lost in our experience of loss.

Elisabeth Kubler-Ross in her *On Death and Dying* lists five stages in the death and dying process. Not only the terminally ill, but also their loved ones go through these five stages: 1. Denial and isolation; 2. Anger; 3. Bargaining; 4. Depression; 5. Acceptance. Let us briefly review these stages, their meaning and their implications for our life.

The first stage, *denial and isolation*, signals the refusal (more or less) of the terminally ill person to believe that she/he is facing death. The personal shock of the news of coming death overwhelms them and us. They deny and try to ignore the stark reality of their disease. They may isolate themselves from others. This stage is usually temporary, and some partial, limited acceptance will replace the initial shock and denial.

The second stage, *anger*, replaces the stance of denial and isolation with the accusatory question and indignant demand, "Why me?" Anger, rage, envy, and resentment are some of the feelings one can experience during this stage. This is a painfully difficult time for medical personnel (doctors, nurses, hospital staff) and for the members of the family and friends. No one understands the plight, understands the helpless and hopeless feelings of the dying person. No one can do anything right for them. Thoroughly frustrated (angry), the terminally ill patient lashes out at others, especially loved ones. Family members and friends are already into their own feelings and emotional experiences regarding their loved one's impending death. They are experiencing their anger too. During this stage, the dying person's expressions of anger can provoke anger and rejection from the very people whom she/he needs at this critical time.

This phase was an especially agonizing time for me and my family during my mother's terminal illness. She became quite angry with us children, to the point of banishing us from her home, banning us from visiting her and from caring for her. She was adamant in her refusal to communicate with us to the point of refusing phone calls and messages. We, too, were caught up in anger — "How could she do this to us?" Three weeks later she died. The week just prior to her death she reconciled with some of us. Unfortunately, I was out of town. My last contact with her was awfully harsh. She refused to speak with me on the phone. As to be expected my grief experience was profoundly compounded and made far more difficult by her refusal. And yet, that awful experience was twelve years ago. As I write and share this experience, my awareness of my profound union in spirit with my mother transcends the negative impact of her refusal long ago. Now I do experience a poignant and present-filled awareness of her, of her spirit with me.

The third stage, *bargaining*, follows the initial denial and anger. The terminally ill person hopes and actively endeavors to merit and to bargain for an extension of life. The hope is that her/his good behavior can earn an extension of life. As children we learned how to bargain for parental permissions. Most of these buying-time bargains and promises are contracted with God. Eventually it becomes obvious that the bargaining is not effective, is not working. The terminally ill person is not getting better.

The fourth stage, *depression*, contains two phases. *Reactive* depression is the grief, guilt, and shame which physical debilitation and incapacity brings. Others have to cover and to substitute for the ill person both at work and at home. The terminally ill person has to let go of past roles and duties. She/he has to sustain even more experiences of helplessness and hopelessness! The other phase is *preparatory* depression; this is future oriented insofar as the patient has to deal with her/his future impending death — the farewell to her/his future in this world and with loved ones. The call during this state is to let go both of one's past involvement as well as one's future involvement in the lives of others.

The fifth stage, *acceptance*, marks a very different experience. The struggle against impending death recedes and dissipates, and there emerges a personal experience of both peace and quietness for the final phase of one's life journey — the journey into life hereafter. The journey inward begins; one displays less interest in talking with and seeing many people. Quiet and silent presence is enough, even relished and savored. Now the dying person possesses her/his spirit in peace and with dignity. Usually at this time the family members and loved ones need more understanding and support than the dying person. They may still be struggling with false hope and bargaining strategies. They, too, are wrestling with the call to let go. They have to confront their resistance in the face of the impending death of a newly resigned and peaceful loved one. The experience of multiple, even conflicting feelings and emotions in the presence of one's death and the death of a loved one are significant for everyone. For within these various feelings and emotions, the presence of God abides. These feelings and emotions, these energies, draw one into the very grief of God. They enable us to participate in the real paradox of the vulnerability of God, the suffering of God, the passion of God. Jurgen Moltmann addresses this paradox in relation to those who experience helplessness and suffering. He writes:

> Anyone who suffers without cause first thinks that he has been forsaken by God. God seems to him to be the mysterious, incomprehensible God who destroys the good fortune that he gave. But anyone who cries out to God in this suffering echoes the death-cry of the dying Christ, the Son of God, who cries with him and intercedes for him with his cross where man in his torment is dumb. . . . God is, God is in us, God suffers in us, where love suffers (*The Crucified God*, pp. 252 and 255).

From experience I have become aware that the death of a loved one in time brings what I call the death-gift. Usually within the year of the death of the loved one, there emerges a new freedom and a new breakthrough within our lives. For each of us some part of life blossoms with new meaning, and this meaning is related to the relationship we enjoyed and released with our loved one. Our own personhood participates in the birth of newness of spirit, newness of direction, newness of purpose and resolve. Somehow the mystery of a death experience is dissolved and transcended within the new mystery of a re-birthing and re-newing reality. This birthing within the year of death is similar to the nine-month period of pregnancy which precedes a child's birth. The death-gift experience is similar to the birth experience, not only in its newness, but also in the period of time required for its emergence.

OUR EXPERIENCES OF OTHER DEATH EVENTS

WE WHO have had to let go of loved ones in and through death, also experience similar feelings and emotional awareness of grief and loss in other events and situations in our life. Some of us have had to let go of relationships with a loved one through irreconcilable conflict and through separation and divorce; sometimes we also have to let go of loved places of residence, loved careers and jobs, and loved experiences of vigorous good health. Kubler-Ross's five stages are also part of our experience and response to these significant losses and changes in our lives. Separation from others or divorce is a death for us; it is the death of friendship or a marital relationship. In divorce it is the death of how a family unit had related to one another. Both of these death experiences change the structure, the context, and the patterns of personal interrelationships. The network of family relationships and friendships shifts and changes and new patterns are called forth from each person involved. This movement out of the old patterns and into the new network is awkward, painful, and ridden with anxiety.

Career changes, new jobs and even promotions can present us with experiences of grief and sadness. The old is gone; the new is upon us. Can we handle this? Residential changes are also accompanied with experiences of grief and loss. Moving to a new home in a different town or city saddens us as we bid farewell to the old and familiar and move on to welcome and to invest ourselves in the new life which awaits us. For us women religious here in the United States, this continual movement in terms of our ministry and residence, our itinerancy, has not only blessed us with the anticipation of the new, but also with the sadness and grief of letting go. Our energy level in going forward to the new call is strongly related to how well we have handled the loss and mourning in terminating the old. The latter energizes the former only to the degree that we enter into the death experience of leaving and letting go in a free and full mature adult manner. In our death experiences, we have to eliminate the after-death expressions just as in birth we have to deal with the release of the after-birth fluids and tissue. Another death-like phenomenon is the empty-nest syndrome which many of us adults have to deal with and handle effectively. Many of us experience this when our children mature, go to college or to work, and then leave home. Our parenting role is over. Our children are no longer ours to direct, to nurture, and to protect. Not only do our children leave our home, but they leave town, leave the state or the country in search of their career and marital commitments. We have to let go, and move on with our lives without them in our space and under our parental care.

Yet another experience of loss that most of us are called to endure is our awareness of our own aging. This experience of our aging carries within it the painful recognition that we are losing our physical vigor and vitality. We witness the diminishing of our physical sensory abilities — our hearing, our sight, our agility and muscle tone; we also experience the changes that creep upon us in terms of hair color, skin texture (wrinkles), weight distribution, and other physiological clues that alert us to the reality that we are not as young as we once were and would like to be. Yes, we encounter more losses to deal with; more calls to let go, and to move on — admittedly a bit more slowly and cautiously. The frailty of the elderly in our midst is a continual reminder to us of the letting go that adult, mature, Christian living calls us to welcome and to embrace.

Grief, sadness, mourning, and loss are personal human experiential energies which need to be released and expressed within our death events and during our periods of mourning, whatever may occasion them. Death experiences are like incisions in that they also bring deep hurt and desolation before they are healed. Moments of death beckon us relentlessly to embark on an inward journey — a journey toward inner healing and inner solace. We make this journey to welcome and to embrace the death reality as both a closure and a beginning of a renewal of life. These death moments also direct us to an outward journey. We are summoned to reach out and to welcome the new and unknown which lay before us, the surprises contained in our personal passage to another way of living and doing. We are invited (sometimes pushed) to move on and to embrace a totally new relationship with self, with others, and with *Abba*-God.

Unfortunately, for some of us, we refuse and we negate the vital new life active within our grief and mourning experiences. We refuse to move or to be moved by these life-giving energies. We become frozen and locked into the anger stage, Kubler-Ross's second stage. We deny and ignore that we are angry — angry at God, angry at our dying loved one for deserting and abandoning us, angry at ourselves for loving, for being so vulnerable and helpless in the presence of the mystery of death. We rebel. We resist. We can spend a lifetime resenting being cut off from a person who means so much to us. We ourselves choose to put our lives into a deep freeze of anger and resentment. We can, and unfortunately do, remain angry, bitter, hostile, and cynical people. Life and God have not treated us either well or fairly. We insist that we deserve better than this, and we demand that we be treated better than this by God. After all, we have obeyed his precepts and followed his law. We assume the personal posture and stance before God and others that we are owed more, we have merited more: "How dare you take this person from me?" We tend to resist, ignore, and deny our inner helplessness in the presence of death. We deny our inner wounding in the presence of death's theft, death's challenge to our rational security, and death's imposition of change upon our planned future. We continue to resist, to ignore, and to deny our inner hurt, our inner wounding, and our inner helplessness present in the face of such a loss. Instead, we rationally and logically appeal to and demand a worldly and cultural justice — "I have a right to expect this person to live, and I demand that this person continue to be part of my life!" We refuse to compromise, to submit, and to accept the reality of death and its personal consequences for our lives.

We, who exhibit this response to significant death experiences, are engaging in fantasy and magic and myth in our expectations and demands regarding life and death. In many instances, these hidden agendas reveal our dreams for happiness, comfort, and self-satisfaction. We are indulging ourselves in fantasy, and we insist on ignoring the reality of life. In a word, these are ego trips. Our expectations (demands) are self-(ego) serving, self-(ego) indulging, and self-(ego) reinforcing. We are into the indulgent Freudian pleasure principle. "I want *what* I want *when* I want it!" Realistic Christian living does not follow this pattern or direction.

OUR INNER DEATH EXPERIENCES

OUR LIVES are marked by both movement and change. Not only are these external, but they are also internal and involve stirrings which occur within our inner world of awareness and experience. Our most profound experiences of sadness, loss, separation, hurt, and grief involve us deeply. We adult Christians engage life in contests and wrestle with ourselves in the process. We, like Jacob in Genesis 32, even take on the angel of our Gospel call, our Gospel invitation, our Gospel summons to repentance and conversion. We struggle, twist and turn backward and forward, and grapple with the angel who pushes us to let go and move on with our Spirit-directed life. We lash out, and are wounded in the course of this inner battle, this inner war. Our inner warfare engages us, wounds us, and even weakens us till, at some point, we lose the taste for battle, and in exhaustion and personal depletion let go and allow to be lost what needs to be last. Then, we limp into our future albeit with new insight, new focus, new purpose, and a new name. We are different. We are changed. Our inner struggles and warfare oftentimes precipitate our grief, our loss, and our wounding.

Doing battle with our inner self is a necessary part of our growth and development into mature adults. Our inner dialogue, our inner turmoil, our inner conflicting voices mesmerize us, lock us into inner frenzy and confusion. "Shall I do this?" "Shall I do that?" "Yes!" "No!" "Maybe, maybe not!" For many of us it is within the realm of our *expectations* that much of our inner battle takes place. Our expectations and our broken dreams can catapult us into many a pit, many a wounded space, many a tortuous position of victimhood and helplessness.

Just what are our expectations? How do they function within us, and how do they manipulate and jeopardize our present life and our future? Most of our expectations flow from egotistical sources and cravings within us. Many of them are childish, unreal, and immature; many of them are ego serving and ego satisfying. Many of them are rooted in our magical thinking and our unreal fantasy life. Our expectations are our position and our posture toward the future. We anticipate with some certitude what others will be and do in future situations and also what we will be and do. This conviction regarding future specific behavior and events can degenerate into narrow control and manipulation. Our expectations can be unreal, even bizarre. We victimize ourselves and often others when we indulge our unreal expectations.

Several years ago, a dear friend of mine decided to change jobs. Sally enjoyed her interviews and perceived her new job as a fantastic opportunity. She accepted the position with a real estate firm, assuming that she would be free to do what she thought needed to be done in the job. My friend is a creative thinker, an energetic woman who enjoys space and freedom in her professional life. During the interview, her supervisor-to-be had given her verbal assurance that she was just the type of professional person their real estate business wanted — a self-activator, an innovative thinker, and a person who respected the input and dignity of her colleagues. Sally was certain that the supervisor-to-be had a lot of trust and faith in her abilities and decision-making skills. Sally became very enthusiastic about her new position and threw herself into the excitement of the challenge.

Well, within a month she began to receive some negative feedback from her supervisor. What she had heard verbally before being hired led her to expect not only agreement from her supervisor, but also affirmation and appreciation of her initiative. Within three months Sally had to face the reality that her supervisor strongly disapproved of her professional procedures and decisions. Sally's work situation became more and more difficult. The professional relationship was deteriorating into an interpersonal struggle. At the end of six months, Sally had reviewed her painful situation; she revised her expectations, re-evaluated her role within the company, and then decided to request a meeting with both her supervisor and the manager of the department in which she was employed. New goals and objectives were discussed. Sally reflected upon these new expectations, decided that they were unrealistic in terms of her approach to working with people, and gave the real estate firm her resignation.

The expectations set up with her supervisor for her work, support, cooperation, and affirmation were only tested on-the-job. Since that painful career experience, Sally's professional life has become more realistic, more creative and productive, and more pleasurable. Through her work experience of the past, she has learned how to manage her expectations of herself and others with greater realism, better communication, and a firmer grasp of the specifics and details in working with others. But Sally had to let go of her fantastic expectations of appreciation and of approval before she could begin to find satisfaction in her work. Letting go of the expectation and the demand that others *have to* appreciate and approve of us is painful.

Most of us need to confront our unreal expectations in three areas of our life: 1) our unreal expectations for others; 2) our response to the unreal expectations which other people place upon us; 3) our own unreal expectations that we impose upon ourselves. We need to reflect upon each of these three areas.

OUR UNREAL EXPECTATIONS FOR OTHERS

THE EXPECTATIONS that we lay upon other adults are really *our* personal demands regarding their persons, their behavior, their decisions and choices. Our expectations (demands), our wishes, our choices are imposed upon others. "How dare they not do what we think they should do! How dare they differ with us who really know what is best for them!" Yes, at times, we do enjoy playing God with the life decisions and life choices of our adult family members and friends. But these expectations are unreal. And our "shoulding" of other adults is blatantly immature, intrusive, and oppressive. Loving someone gives us neither the right nor the duty to control, to dominate, or to manipulate their life. Loving someone does not mean that we know what is best for her/him. Our letting go of our ego-need and our ego-desire to control and to manipulate the lives of people we love entails much wrestling with the oppressive, personal forces within us. Surrendering our judgmental stance in relation to others signifies a genuine Gospel conversion for most of us. Letting go of our one-upmanship and our overseer posture initiates us into a new, adult way of relating with others. We could spare ourselves much grief and hurt if we would continue to care for others and yet let go of our we-know-what-is-best-for-you stance in relation to them. The most that we can expect from others is that they will do what *they* need to do, what *they* perceive themselves needing to do. We must trust the decisions and choices that others make.

From my own life experiences I have learned that we function out of three basic energy sources: 1) political; 2) psychological; and 3) spiritual. Our *political* energy base is characterized by agreement and/or disagreement. Our opinion polling and political voting processes depend upon agreement and disagreement in the projection of where people stand in relation to issues and to the selection of candidates. For some of us, agreement with and affirmation from others is crucial in our relationships. We expect and, indeed, demand that others agree with our opinions, our ideas, and our choices. For us, agreement is personal acceptance; disagreement is personal rejection. Our posture of always expecting and always demanding agreement can become unreal, even bizarre. Difference is only difference unless we choose to inflate it with personal negation, personal rejection, and personal abandonment. Each of us is different, and conflict and diversity of opinions, ideas, and lifestyles are to be expected. When we demand agreement from others, especially in the name or under the guise of loyalty, we are involved in tyrannical, oppressive behavior. We cannot demand uniformity of opinion and conformity of behavior from other adults. When we do, we are exposing our own clone-prone behavior; we are demanding that others identify with, reflect, and express our opinions, our postures, and our choices. Others, too, need to live within their own integrity, their own self-truth. For mature adults to be energized by political power and motivation not emanating from within, but exerted by forces and pressures outside themselves is inadequate and insufficient; in fact, such an overposturing influence is dehumanizing. We cannot enjoy mature, humane relationships with others if we insist upon locking them into agreement with our opinions regarding them and their lives. Letting go of our demand for agreement is painful for us. In so doing, we give others the freedom to be and to become whom *Abba*-God intends them to be and to become. Our culture and our world are addicted to conformity and to uniformity; and both of these addictions are rooted in agreement. Older adults tend to demand agreement more than younger adults.

Our *psychological* power source is characterized by understanding and misunderstanding. Especially in our age of anxiety is our demand to be understood more emphatic and pronounced. Younger adults tend to demand to be understood more than older adults. Understanding other persons, their joy and sadness, is rarely encountered. Who really understands the recesses of the human heart? No one. Only *Abba*-God knows and cherishes us from a perspective and a posture that look deep within. It is true, that we may have experiences of joy and sadness that are similar to others, yet complete understanding is still lacking. Similarity of experience is only similarity of experience. No two experiences are identical. We can and like to imagine what another is experiencing, yet full awareness is never possible. Again, we are called by the Gospel to let go of both our demand to be understood and our demand to understand completely what others are experiencing. Each of us resembles an iceberg with only the tip of our personhood revealing itself. The vast, unseen, hidden, yet powerful depths of our self-mystery function beneath the conscious, observable surface. Mature living demands that we get in contact and in communication with our depths, with our hidden yet potent dimensions.

Our third source of power and energy is *spiritual* and it calls us to trust. Yes, we can choose and we can decide to trust the *differing* other, even though we neither agree with nor understand her/him. Mature, adult behavior insists upon trust — trusting the person who is different from us and whom we do not pretend to understand. Our trust stance gives others the permission and the freedom to be and to become all they can be and become. Our trust is our affirmation of the unique dimensions which God's creative action possesses. Each of us, created and coming from God's loving hand, is unique, singular, one-of-a-kind. Trusting the differing other in her/his difference is a God-like way of relating to another. Letting go of our demands for agreement and understanding makes us more vulnerable in the presence of our own uniqueness and the uniqueness of others.

OUR RESPONSE TO THE UNREAL EXPECTATIONS OF OTHERS

ONE OF THE MOST PAINFUL TURNING POINTS in adult living is the movement away from having to please others, having to have the approval of others, and having to conform our behavior to the norms and standards of others. At some point each of us has to cut the cord of approval which binds us to others. We are afraid of other people's disapproval. We are afraid that they will not like us. The approval and disapproval of others can intimidate, even scare us at times. Others are guilty of exercising false and unreal expectations in regard to us. They can demand forms of behavior from us at times which make them feel good, but which have no meaning or purpose for us. The old story about the adult who feels chilly and then insists that the child put on a sweater is pertinent here. Part of our growing up is letting go of the unreal expectations that we are subjected to by others. We do have the power to accept or to reject these unreal expectations. The Gospel calls and invites us to activate and to act upon our real expectations, to hear and to implement our self-truth, and to trust our inner voice, our inner direction and inspiration. Our own integrity and our own self-truth depend upon this trust, this surrender to our inner guide and support. Our struggle to be and to function as women and men of personal conviction and personal commitment presents a formidable challenge in our culture today. We have many social and political forces pressing us to conform to popular opinions and beliefs.

Our adult, mature way of following Christ Jesus summons us to listen, to hear, and to respond to our inner promptings, to the Spirit within each of us. Each of us has to discover the new world *within* us. In our youth when we studied geography, we were taught about the seven continents; we learned about the people, the products, and the climate which influenced both the people and their culture. We now have to embark upon our individual journey of discovery and establish claim to our own land, our "eighth continent." Each of us has to "Go inward!" Each of us has to discover the world, the continent, the universe, the land of promise *within* us. We have squatter's rights to this territory. Our task involves naming it, claiming it, and taming it. Within us resides the energy and the direction for our mature adult being and becoming. We are called to care for this land of promise just as Adam and Eve and the Israelites were told to cherish and nurture their gift of land. Our "blossoming and blooming" depends upon how well we are rooted within our interior world and how well we are watered from our inner springs and fountains. This shift from dependence and reliance upon external support and direction to dependence and reliance upon our internal voices and soundings entails or demands a radical conversion. At the time of conversion we shift from exterior, social conformity to interior, inner listening and personal freedom rooted in our own self-truth. This conversion time, this adult task, can be awfully painful. Letting go of our dependence upon other people, letting go of endeavoring to please other people, letting go of our empowerment of other people and other opinions produces its own trauma. It can resemble the trauma of birth, of being delivered, of being freed from our chains and bondage to others. Our "birthing" ushers us into our new world which demands that we initiate reaching out, mobility, and interaction with others. Our fetal posture is past; our active embrace of our life and the life of others calls us to a different stance. Furthermore, we are expected to stand erect before God and others. We take responsibility for our lives, for our involvements with others, and for the movements and soundings which direct and bless our life.

UNREAL EXPECTATIONS THAT WE IMPOSE UPON OURSELVES

ANOTHER SOURCE of immature and childish anxiety that we often experience is the grief which we heap upon ourselves in and through our own unreal expectations and demands.

Many of us assume that anything and everything that we do has to and must be perfect, that is, without flaw. There is an unconscious presupposition that perfection and unattainable standards of excellence are the norm and the standard for our behavior and achievement. Needless to say, we fail to meet and to live up to these unrealistic goals. And we give ourselves over to needless experiences of fear, guilt, and shame. We choose to feel miserable. And the more miserable we are, the more some of us seem to enjoy the misery. Letting go of our expectations and our demands which fill us with guilt and fear frees us to trust more in our interior voice and inspiration. Our ego does not release its control and power over us too easily. It will fight and battle us for the power to intimidate and control us through fear and guilt. Our letting go of our fear, guilt, and shame frees us from inflicting upon ourselves our own punitive and our own bullying behavior. Our theology of creation tells us that we are created from the loving hand of *Abba*-God; we are graced people with God-like beauty and power; we deserve to care for, to reverence who we are from God, and we deserve to praise and give thanks to *Abba*-God for creating us in his image. Self-loathing, self-punishment, and self-condemnation are not adult Christian actions. They are not loving actions and responses. Learning to love ourselves in the way that *Abba*-God loves us is the mandate which every adult Christian has to grapple with in the course of her/his lifetime. Our affirmation of who we are (our inner continent), where we are going (our growth in love), and how we are behaving (our inner likeness to the person of Christ Jesus) requires from us joy, peace, patience, and trust in the Spirit within us and within others.

OUR EXPRESSIONS OF SADNESS, GRIEF AND LOSS

MANY OF US are uncomfortable with sharing and expressing our grief and sadness with others. Men in our culture are especially hesitant to own and to claim that they are hurting, that they are grieving. Much of what passes for anger in men's feeling and emotional expressions is really hurt and grief. Each of us needs to review and to assess how we deal with the grief and the mourning experiences within our lives. Adult Christian living calls us to be at ease with our expressions of grief and mourning. In addition, many of us are not at ease with other people's expressions of grief, sadness, and hurt. Our experiences of hurt and grief are real; our expressions of these human experiences are also real. Especially do we need to be gentle and tender with ourselves when we are suffering grief and mourning experiences. Our first response and expression in relation to ourselves is compassion, tenderness and gentleness with our wounded state. This is a prerequisite for subsequent healing. Many of us tend to be harsh and cruel with ourselves when we are hurting and grieving deeply. I have found in my own experience that many people who are empathetic with others in their grief can be exceptionally cruel and hostile to themselves when they are in deep pain. For some of us, to be in pain and in sorrow is to be less than what we were, to be weak. Human vulnerability is perceived as a liability. We fail to realize that human vulnerability is the cornerstone of much that supports adult Christian spirituality. Charles Peguy's famous line, "All life comes from tenderness" (*God Speaks*) is appropriate in terms of our healing and our renewal after a deeply wounding death experience, a deeply poignant experience of suffering.

Another dimension of being at ease with our expression of grief and sadness is our freedom to weep. There are some pains that cannot be healed without the cleansing of the wound by the tears which inundate both the human psyche and the human soul. Weeping can be cleansing. Weeping can be cathartic. In our culture many men do not possess this freedom to weep. They refuse themselves the permission to express the grief, the hurt, and the loss they are experiencing so profoundly. Our weeping elicits a very tender and gentle movement from within each of us. It is difficult for a human to become humane without some weeping at significant times in life. Many men whom I have worked with in spiritual direction and psychotherapy have come to me with gallons of tears within them. Many of these men described themselves as angry. And yet upon discussion much of their alleged anger was unclaimed hurt and sadness. Men have to grieve too. Our culture gives women many more permissions for weeping when experiencing grief, sadness, and hurt.

Our grief and sadness usually calls us into some silence and withdrawal. This expression of our grief makes our friends and family somewhat uncomfortable at times. The deeper and more profound the grief and the experience of loss and mourning, the greater is the need for private time, for quiet, and for some withdrawal from the normal hubbub of daily life. Our need to grieve at times can resemble our medical need for intensive care. The deeper parts of ourselves which are wounded need quiet, inactive healing time. Personal energies need to be channelled into our innermost self rather than being spent in active, extroverted types of behavior and activities. For some of us our grief time is root-healing time. We need to attend to our grief and loss needs if we expect to heal and to move on with our lives. Extra rest, more sleep, more leisure can be quite soothing and helpful. Beauty is very healing for us during times of deep grief: listening to music, reading favorite pieces of poetry, being present to certain Scriptural passages, spending more time with nature — in the park and at the lake, taking walks in the country — are also healing activities. Beauty has the power to touch us, to heal us at the deepest levels of our being, and during our time of sorrowing we need the balm of beauty to soothe and to help us.

The Scriptures remind us over and over again, that *Abba*-God heals the brokenhearted, and hears their pleas. Both in the Hebrew and in the Christian Scriptures, God's presence to his people who are suffering is proclaimed. They groaned then; we groan today. At times our human situation is terribly painful and grief stricken. Psychologists and psychiatrists try to help us control our lives and our life situations, and yet there are factors beyond our control which are painful for each of us. Working with and through our pain with sincerity and truth is the challenge that the Gospel presents to each adult Christian woman and man. We cannot avoid loss, sadness, mourning, and hurt. Encountering these experiences without expressions of self-loathing, self-hatred, and self-condemnation is the goal of mature, Christian spirituality, mature Gospel living.

Suffering is a universal human experience. Human pain is present at every time, in every era, in every culture. Each culture has in some way dreamed of the time when suffering would be abolished. We Christians look forward to the Parousia, the Second Coming of Christ Jesus. We look forward to the Second Coming to abolish human suffering, to complete the fullness of the Kingdom of Peace, the Kingdom of Justice, the Kingdom of Love. As we know, the Christian Scriptures close with this longing, this hope, "Come, Lord Jesus!"

SUMMARY

SADNESS, GRIEF, MOURNING, AND LOSS are experiences with which each of us has had some contact, some awareness of within the recent past. Suffering is a universal human experience. Central to the experience of pain and suffering is the struggle we humans have in not losing ourselves in the suffering experience. Self-absorption is the great temptation buried in the quicksand of grief, sadness, mourning, and loss. Self-transcendence rather than self-absorption is the healthy and Christian resolution of human suffering. Death experiences and death-like experiences bring us into times of grief, loss, hurt, and/or suffering. People come into our lives, change and modify them and our response to life; they also leave our lives through death, through distance in space and in time, and through diversity in interests and lifestyle. We experience sadness and separation. We grieve; we mourn; we hurt; we suffer. Our sadness is the grief, mourning, and loss we experience in letting go, bidding farewell, and having to move on.

Elisabeth Kubler-Ross lists five stages in the death and dying process which both terminally ill patients and their loved ones experience. These are: 1) Denial and isolation; 2) Anger; 3) Bargaining; 4) Depression; 5) Acceptance. These stages can also accompany other death-like experiences such as: separation and divorce; estrangement from family and loved ones; change in residence; job loss and career changes; and aging. These death-like experiences precipitate sadness, loss, grief, hurt, and suffering.

Inner-death experiences occur in our lives as well as the observable, external deaths and losses. Letting go of our unreal expectations can be compared to intensive heart surgery for us. Yes, we have to let go, cut out, and cut off controlling the lives of others with our unreal expectations, and being controlled by the unreal expectations of others. Severing control initiates a painful period for each of us. I believe it is comparable to the heart surgery spoken of by Ezekiel (11 and 36) and Jeremiah (31). This heart surgery, this heart transplant, disrupts our lives, distances us from our past, and places us on the road to an unknown and unfamiliar future. Letting go and moving on can be quite painful for us. Our Gospel call reiterates God's call to let go of our servitude to the approval and disapproval of others. The God within, the God within our "eighth continent" awaits us, awaits our presence, and awaits our making our home within the inscape of our self-truth. Our land of promise awaits our care, our cultivation, and our enjoyment of its riches.

Our most difficult and painful letting go is our having to surrender, our having to release, and our having to abandon our pet fears, our pet guilt, and our pet shame. Through our fear, guilt, and shame, we give ourselves permission to punish, to abuse, and to condemn ourselves. We ignore the forgiveness, the compassion, and the patience which adult Christian women and men can bring to human fear, guilt, and shame.

FOUR

Anger And Christian Integrity

INTRODUCTION

ANGER, ITS EXPERIENCE AND ITS EXPRESSION, is a remarkably fascinating and intriguing feeling and emotion. Just when we assume that we have an understanding of our own anger process, a new awareness surprises us. Whenever we are experiencing ourselves as constricted and helpless in a given situation, we can assume that anger in some form and to some degree is present. As in other feelings and emotions, anger has a varied range and depth. Our human psyche can be compared to a large-size swimming pool. Our pool has shallow and deep places within its borders. So too, our experiences of anger can be of different depths and intensities. Annoyance differs from fury as boredom differs from rage or wrath. Our one-foot anger experiences differ considerably from our nine-foot anger experiences. What is anger? Anger is that feeling or emotion which emerges when we feel threatened, overpowered, and rendered helpless, when we feel we are without control, without power, without autonomy. The Indo-European root word, *angh*, means constricted, narrow, tight, squeezed. Anger is the feeling which accompanies being pressured, limited shrunk. These feelings — frustration, resentfulness, revenge, indignation, fury, retaliation, hostility, wrath — come in varying degrees and intensity.

Anger is a commonplace feeling in our current culture. There is much in contemporary life, especially in our work life, which evokes both frustration and annoyance. Urban living is hectic and overpowering for many of us. Coping with the noise level on our streets, finding parking places when we have to do business, dealing with appointments for our medical problems, enjoying some social life with others, meeting with financial, legal, and educational personnel at times convenient for them — all of these necessary actions make us feel utterly helpless. Many of our daily life experiences at work involve annoyance, irritation, even rage. How do we deal with these feelings and emotions? And yet, our feelings of anger are essential for the maintenance of healthy adult behavior. Our expressions of anger are part of the full range of human emotions that we as adults need to be capable of both experiencing and expressing. The evil in society that we adult Christians have to deal with can induce anger-related feelings and emotions. Our culturally fostered sense of competition, alienation, domination, and superwoman/superman expectations lead us into much that can trigger off anger-related behavior. Willard Gaylin in *The Rage Within* reflects at length upon our modern encounters with an anger-provoking society.

Several months ago I was in New York City for a weekend business visit. Twice I took cabs to get where I had to meet with my colleagues. In both instances, the cab drivers were angry men. One of them burst into rage at one point shouting his feelings at the drivers in the other cars as he darted crazily in and out of the traffic through Manhattan. I sat in the back seat, frightened and intimidated as I listened to him rant and rave. I felt quite relieved when I reached my destination. No one of us today can escape experiencing anger or participating in someone else's expression of it.

OUR EXPERIENCES OF ANGER

ANGER IS TO CHRISTIAN LIFE what elimination is to healthy physical well-being. All living organisms participate in intake-output processes; all living organisms have to concern themselves with both nourishment and elimination. Anger has to do with the elimination of the waste, the excess, the non-integrated experiences of our life. Our remarks in the face of a frustrating situation, "Who needs this?" "I don't need this!" can be our way of refusing the uncomfortable situation. Each of us needs to have ways and means of draining off and eliminating our helpless and hopeless experiences. Feelings of anger cannot be denied, negated, ignored, displaced, suppressed, or rationalized without a toxic buildup within our psyche and within our spirit life. We encounter many situations and circumstances in our lives that we find hard to accept and to digest without discomfort and resentment. These feelings of conflict and resistance to reality often manifest themselves in outbursts of frustration, resentment, and anger. Even though we try to mask these feelings behind a serene, calm, and cool facade and at times even try to bury and deny them, they do affect our behavior. These anger-related feelings emerge when we least expect them, often surfacing in negative and hostile ways. They can surprise and alarm us. In truth, we begin functioning as constipated spirits. Our responses to new situations become closed and pessimistic; we expect the worst; we perceive ourselves as victims locked into constricted and pressured life situations. Our buried past anger sours our present experiences and cuts off any fresh and open approach to the future. We become depressed, de-energized, and dejected. Merely to survive is our sole short-sighted goal. We lose our appetite for life. We have no *joie de vivre!* Life becomes a drag, a bore.

OUR EXPRESSIONS OF ANGER

IN OUR CULTURE, expressions of anger are a problem for many of us. Women, for example are usually not given permission to express anger. "Be ladylike!" is an important mandate we women receive from both women and men alike. For many of us, expressions of anger are a "No-No." Women are still expected to be calm, to surrender to and to accept any type of treatment, and not express indignation and anger. Both women and men give permission to men to express their anger more freely and more frequently. And yet anger is a human experience common to both women and men. Both need to learn to express it in a humane, adult manner.

Central to the consideration of human anger is our awareness that there is an ethic, a morality governing the expression of anger. Human elimination has its "how-to's" and its "how-not-to's." Just as each of us in childhood experienced norms and were given specific guidelines in our toilet training, so later in life, we need to review and to evaluate how to eliminate and express our anger in a constructive, mature, life-giving manner. As adults we need to engage in ethical and wholesome psychological and spiritual anger training behaviors. In childhood *how*, *when*, and *where* were important realities in our toilet training. So, too, in our anger expressions as adults, *how*, *when*, and *where* are important in sharing, expressing, and eliminating our anger. We do not have permission to "do it" in any way and anywhere we please. Both the individual and social consequences of our expressions of anger have to be taken into consideration. Others have the right to be treated and related to with respect and dignity even in the face of our anger. To reduce others to objects of our anger (to make them toilets) is destructive and unethical. Scapegoating others when we are angry dehumanizes them, and we are accountable to others for this destructive behavior. We need to remember that when we are angry, we *do* have choices. We can make decisions. The issue is not whether we express or do not express our anger. The real issue is *how* we choose to express our anger.

Obviously, it is necessary that we in truth name and claim our anger. For many of us, this is difficult because we have conditioned ourselves to deny the reality of our anger. We women tend to deny our feelings of anger more than men do. In my ministry with women in retreat work and spiritual direction, I have had many women come to me with little or no awareness that they are angry and resentful. They complain of being bored, of feeling empty, of experiencing no desire for prayer. Their spirits are impacted and constipated with buried, unreleased, and denied anger. They are nauseated with life, and do not experience themselves as being nourished by their life involvements. My first task is to enable them to become aware of their need to name and claim their past anger. Only then can they deal with letting go, eliminating their past, buried, impacted feelings of anger.

Every sophisticated and organized culture has procedures and strategies for (1) the gathering and (2) the disposal of waste, of garbage, of sewage. These two processes, the gathering and the disposal, are each necessary and fundamental to the personal health of an individual and also to the social health of a community. These two processes are also important in terms of our elimination of feelings and emotions of anger. Merely to gather together our garbage, our waste, is insufficient. In our contemporary life, we have all of us experienced garbage strikes in our towns and cities. The heaps of garbage left in our homes or out on the streets do not solve the waste problem. Stacked up indoors or out on the streets for indefinite periods of time, it simply creates more problems. The possibility of disease becomes imminent for the individual and for the neighborhood and civic community. The second process, the disposal of the waste, the garbage, is also necessary. Without removal and disposal, the accumulated garbage can become a health hazard. Our modern toilet is an excellent image of these two processes. The toilet bowl collects, gathers the waste, and the lever when pressed flushs away and disposes of it. Some of us refuse to press the lever. We refuse to let go of our feelings and emotions of anger. We can become addicted to our accumulation of waste, of bitter and resentful feelings.

For many of us our addiction to alcohol, drugs, smoking, food, are expressions of our collected past anger. We can become the dark clouds, the wet blankets, the wimps that darken, dampen, and discourage any joy and life-delight in our personal and social situations. We become the prophets of doom and gloom among the people with whom we live and work. For me, Job on his dunghill with his three "moaners" accurately portrays the constipated spirit, the angry and indignant person. It was only after his ventilation, the release and elimination of his angry feelings and emotions, that healing and a realistic personal renewal did occur within him and with his God. So it is that we need to gather (name and claim in truth) our waste, and then dispose and eliminate our feelings of past and buried anger and resentment. Each of us has strong feelings regarding our past helplessness and victimhood that we need to own and then eliminate. Each of us needs to be healed of these past feelings of injustice and woundedness that we cling to. We need to press the lever! We need to flush the toilet!

STRATEGIES FOR EXPRESSING OUR ANGER IN A MATURE MANNER

OUR COMMITMENT TO TRUTH, our Christian integrity, summons us to encounter our anger in a forthright and humane manner. Our anger needs to be dealt with in a mature, constructive way. Our feelings of anger are real. They ask to be acknowledged and recognized by us with genuine compassion and acceptance. Perhaps making a list of persons and events in the past that evoked our anger can be of help in owing our feelings. Merely to feel angry, to name and claim our anger, is not wrong, is not sinful. Our candid awareness of our anger and our gentle embrace of our buried, past angry feelings are our first steps in our healing process. Owning our feelings of resentment and hostility is owning the way we still feel about a person or event in our past. It says nothing about the objective situation or the person. It affirms only our feelings about the situation or person. Our feelings are only *our* feelings concerning the objective person, place, or event. My buried past feelings of anger toward a person or an event are only my feelings. It is very important to realize that when I have negative feelings toward another person or situation, my feelings do not make that person or situation evil, ugly, or destructive. My angry feelings do not magically transform others into monsters and ghouls. People are who they are irrespective of how I feel toward them.

Many of us operate out of childish remnants of magic and fantasy. We can have strong anger-related feelings toward people whom we dearly love, people who are fine, caring, Christian women and men. Our feelings reveal more about us (and our ego demands) than they do about other persons, places, and events. Some of us are afraid to own our feelings because we fear that our feelings are condemnations and rejections of other people's integrity and character. We need to be aware that we can name and claim our angry feelings and still not stand in judgment and condemnation of another. Mature, adult behavior can distinguish between feelings of anger (our ego demands) and another person's integrity and virtue.

When naming and claiming our buried past feelings of anger, we need to focus in upon how we experienced ourselves as diminished, put down, and wounded in the situation. First, we need to explore this anger within ourselves. Some people find it helpful to write it out. Second, some people find it helpful to form an image of how they felt during the painful situation. "I felt like: a dog, a worm, a door mat, a piece of trash, a slave, a fool." Whatever the image that surfaces, listen to it, feel it, allow it to pass through us, and out of us — drain it off. In most instances, we wanted some different kind of treatment from the person or the situation. Are we willing to let go of and to release our desires, our expectations, and our demands for specific treatment from the person or situation? If not, we are still hanging on to *our* demand, *our* way in the past situation. William Johnston writes: "When anger arises in the heart from the frustration of not getting what we want, then the worst possible thing is to deny it, repress it, pretend it is not there. 'I'm not angry. Ha! Ha!' For this is to ram it into the unconscious where it will fester, causing acute depression or exploding in some unforeseen way. Much better then, to recognize it and tell your friends about it" (*Christian Mysticism Today*, p. 57).

Speaking with someone else about the anger and the resentment can also be helpful. We reveal our own vulnerability when we share with another our feelings of resentment and frustration. In sharing these past feelings, we need to consciously express them as our own. We must speak in the first person: *I* feel resentful; *I* feel disgusted; *I* am angry about what happened three years ago. In so doing we are asserting how we feel, and we are not aggressively accusing another or striking out in a condemning way towards another. In expressing our feelings we are sharing how *we* feel, not dumping negative accusations on another person. We are sharing data about how *we* are experiencing the other person, the past situation. For many of us, we learned immature anger expressions from watching and hearing other people "chew out" both others and us when they were angry. Attacking others is immature, childish, emotional behavior — mere temper tantrums. Mature expressions of anger do not have to be blaming, condemning diatribes against others. Such behavior is hostile, abusive, and ethically wrong. It is not Christian adult emotional behavior. Such behavior is cruel. We cannot condone and indulge abusive angry behavior.

Another very effective way to drain off feelings and emotions of anger is physical exercise. Daily exercise is a tremendous way to help the body — and consequently the whole person — eliminate the physical effects of stress and anger. Walking a mile or two a day is an excellent way of getting the physical exercise that we need. Other people find that biking and jogging drains off the tightness and the muscle tension within the body that anger-related feelings can precipitate. Playing tennis and golf are other fine ways of working off and working out the constriction and tightness within our muscles. More and more of us are participating in jazzercise, aerobics, and other group and music-accompanied fitness programs. Furthermore, there are a variety of self-help programs on the market that we can use right in our own home. Frequent exercise is a must not only for physical well-being, but also for sound and sane psychological health.

ANGER AND OUR CHRISTIAN LIFE

THE SCRIPTURES, both Hebrew and Christian, give ample testimony to our need to eliminate the waste, the garbage, the anger in our life. They provide us with many situations wherein both the human experience and the expressions of anger are valid, even sacred. We can identify with the Biblical experiences of anger and its expression and really learn how the holy women and men of God experienced and expressed their anger in their personal and social life situations.

The Psalms in the Hebrew Scriptures provide us with numerous examples and instances of this. The psalmist places himself before Yahweh in a childlike posture, pouring out all his feelings of woundedness and hostility with openness and candor. The intense lyrical quality of these expressions of anger is startling, disarming, even shocking to us cool, contained, and controlled Westerners in our modern technological world. The anger Psalms express strong feelings of resentment, rage, desire for retaliation, revenge, curses, and the desire for justice. Nothing is held in or held back. The psalmist expresses it all and quite vehemently to Yahweh who cares for and protects the interests as well as the person of the psalmist. Once the psalmist unloads all of his angry feelings and emotions, he assumes and concludes that now it is God's business, God's problem to solve, God's duty to repair the damage. The psalmist is freed of it; the psalmist is clean, empty of it all, and now he can get on with his life. What the psalmist is really doing is *entrusting* all of his anger regarding the personal injustice and injury to Yahweh, the God of power and might, who will take care of it for him. The psalmist trusts Yahweh's active care and concern for him.

Whenever I read and pray with the anger Psalms, I imagine a young child running to a nurturing and protective parent to scream about what another child, a playmate, has done to her/him. The hurt and angry child wants the parent to punish the mean and wounding playmate. The hurt and angry child wants the parent to take charge of the situation, to render justice, and to re-establish peace, balance, and harmony. The parental "I'll take care of it" frees the child from the experience of helplessness and victimhood. Comforting the injured and angry child is the first way the parent does justice and takes care of the pained and hurting youngster. The comforting and reassuring parent brings justice to the situation insofar as the parent gives the child what she/he needs at this moment — reassurance that she/he is loved, is lovable. So it is that the psalmist — with that remarkable child-like, crystal-clear candor and simplicity — shares it all with Yahweh, who loves him. The hurt and pain are too much for the child-like psalmist who in effect says, "It's too much for me. You take charge. You handle the offender. And by the way, I have a few suggestions about what you can do to punish him!"

The tremendous differences between the psalmist and me are: First, the psalmist is constantly aware of Yahweh with him throughout the entire anger experience and its expression. By contrast with the psalmist, when I am feeling really angry, usually much of the intensity of my own anger is related to my perception that I am utterly alone in my experience of helplessness and vulnerability. Many times, my faith in *Abba*-God's presence is weak, so that for me *Abba*-God is not perceived as there for me to unload on and scream out to for help and delivery. And second, after the psalmist entrusts and unloads all his angry feelings onto God, he is free and clean. On the other hand, I tend to cling to my anger, and want to retaliate, to punish my "enemy" myself. The psalmist gives all of this to Yahweh. It continually amazes me how intimately the psalmist both experiences the presence of

Yahweh and freely expresses his feelings and emotions of anger to Yahweh. How trusting and transparent the child-like psalmist is with the God of his youth!

There are several psalms which exemplify the psalmist's childlike trust, candor, and anger in the presence of Yahweh, his God. Psalms 58 and 59 reflect the hurt and anger of the wounded psalmist. Especially do we see the hurt and the revenge-filled psalmist in Psalm 109. First, the psalmist approaches Yahweh with trust and assurance:

> O God, whom I praise, be not silent,
> > for they have opened wicked and treacherous mouths
> > > against me.
> They have spoken to me with lying tongues,
> > and with words of hatred they have encompassed me
> > > and attacked me without cause.
> In return for my love they slandered me,
> > but I prayed.
> They repaid me evil for good
> > and hatred for my love (Ps 109:1-5).

Now, the psalmist begins to recommend and suggest to God how to punish his enemies and re-establish order and balance. The curses he comes up with are strong and devastating in their call for revenge and retribution.

> Raise up a wicked man against him,
> > and let the accuser stand at his right hand.
> When he is judged, let him go forth condemned,
> > and may his pleas be in vain.
> May his days be few;
> > may another take his office.
> May his children be fatherless,
> > and his wife a widow.

Anger and Christian Integrity

> May his children be roaming vagrants and beggars;
> > may they be cast out of the ruins of their homes.
> May the usurer ensnare all his belongings,
> > and strangers plunder the fruit of his labors.
> May there be no one to do him a kindness,
> > nor anyone to pity his orphans.
> May his posterity meet with destruction;
> > in the next generation may their name be blotted out
> > > (Ps 109:6-13).

And so it goes with these vehement and merciless expressions of anger! And yet, the psalmist ends again with thanksgiving and trust in his God.

> I will speak my things earnestly to the Lord,
> > and in the midst of the throng I will praise him,
> For he stood at the right hand of the poor man,
> > to save him from those who would condemn him
> > > (Ps 109:30-32).

The Christian Scriptures also provide us with other examples of experiences and expressions of anger. They give us wholesome models of women and men who needed to eliminate this kind of waste and garbage from their lives. Jesus was a man who understood the human need for adult, mature anger. Early on in his ministry, he was confronted with the passive-aggressive behavior of the Scribes and Pharisees. Both their addiction to legalism and their anxiety regarding his emphasis upon the need of people as superior to the law, and also the positive response of the people to him engendered both suspecion and hostility within them. When Jesus cured the man with a withered hand on the Sabbath in Mark 3:1-6, aware that the Scribes and Pharisees were watching him in order to bring legal charges against him, he called the man out of the crowd to stand in front of the group. Then he directed a legal question to the Scribes and Pharisees about whether the law or human life was primary. They ducked his question. They stood in silence — the silence of distance and disengagement. They squeezed him out, walled him out with their stone silence. And he knew it. The Gospel writer tells us, "He looked around at them with anger, for he was deeply grieved that they had closed their minds against him." Jesus told the man standing in front of the crowd to stretch out his arm, and then he cured his withered hand. And the enemies of Jesus left together and together started to plan and to plot how they would destroy him. Another classic example of Jesus' anger is depicted in the incident when he threw the people out of the temple area who were there engaged in commerce. This cleansing of the temple is related in Mark 11: 15-18. Again, we see Jesus experiencing anger fully and expressing it freely. Both expressions (that of the man with the withered hand and the temple episode) were direct and forthright.

Mary, the mother of Jesus, also gives us an example of exasperation and frustration in the story of Jesus lost in the temple in Luke 2:41-52. After searching in vain for three days for the young twelve-year-old boy, Mary and Joseph find him in the temple. Mary's "Why have you done this to us?" for me has always meant, "How could you do this to us?" For me, she portrays any frustrated and annoyed person searching and not finding a loved one, even searching for and not finding the Lord — a very heart-rending and provoking experience!

In our Christian life, anger is a powerful and dynamic force in terms of our response to social injustice and inhumanity toward others. For adult, mature Christians this call to justice is a call to redress the wrongs and indignities which social and national groups inflict upon the weak, the poor, the minorities, and the others who are different. Many of us prefer to sympathize or identify with the cowardly silence of the distanced and the disengaged rather than to speak out and take action with Christian indignation in defense of the oppressed and the bullied. Christian indignation has an important Gospel role to play in the life and spirituality of mature, adult Christian women and men.

Charity is the fruit of the tree of justice. Without justice, charity is a sham, a guilt trip, an ego balm for the oppressor. St. Augustine realized this, and attributed to the virtue of hope a higher priority than he gave to charity. He writes that the virtue of hope has two daughters, Anger and Courage. Anger is the daughter who says "No" to what must not be, to what must not continue to become. Enough is enough! And Courage is the daughter who says "Yes" to what needs to be, to what needs to become. Christian indignation, our Gospel prophetic call and stance, speaks to and takes action in terms of what needs to be stopped, what needs to be terminated, and also what needs to be initiated, what needs to be begun with courage and with justice. Christian indignation calls us to Gospel responsibility and to Gospel accountability. We cannot ignore either; we cannot remain silent and inactive in the face of any form of inhumanity to other human beings, in the face of injustice to our weak, despairing and alienated sisters and brothers. Christian solidarity with the poor and the oppressed is the mark of our mature, adult, Christian spirituality. We are one. Schillebeeckx goes so far as to suggest in his interpretation of Matthew 25, that each person's well-being is God's will, God's affair. The poor person is the one who judges us, for in Jesus, God identified himself with the poor and the oppressed. If we enjoy solidarity with the poor, the poor themselves will invite us into the heavenly kingdom. According to Schillebeeckx, (*God Is New Each Moment*, pp. 31-32), it will be the poor themselves who will welcome us with,

"Come. You have my Father's blessing! Inherit the kingdom prepared for you from the creation of the world. For I was hungry and you gave me food, I was thirsty and you gave me drink. I was a stranger and you welcomed me, naked and you clothed me. I was ill and you comforted me, in prison and you came to visit me" (Mt 25:33-36).

SUMMARY

ANGER is the feeling or emotion which emerges when we feel threatened, overpowered, helpless, out of control, without authority, and without personal autonomy. These feelings vary in degree and intensity. In our contemporary life and culture, especially at work, there are many forces and factors which can precipitate feelings of helplessness and hopelessness within us. Our experiences and expressions of anger are part of the full range of human feelings and emotions that we as adults need to be capable of both experiencing and expressing.

Anger is to Christian life what elimination is to physical well-being. All living organisms have to deal with both nourishment and elimination. Anger has to do with the elimination of the waste, the excess, the non-integrated experiences of our life. Each of us needs to have ways and means of draining off and eliminating our helpless and hopeless experiences. Feelings of anger cannot be denied, negated, ignored, displaced, suppressed, or rationalized without a toxic buildup in our psyche and our spirit life.

In our culture, expressions of anger are a problem for many of us. Women are usually not given permission to express anger. Men are more readily allowed to express anger. In childhood, *how, when,* and *where* were important guidelines in our toilet training. So too, in our expressions of anger as adults, *how, when,* and *where* are important guidelines for expressing our anger. We do not have permission to "do it" to anyone in any way and anywhere we please. Others have the right to be treated and related to with respect and dignity even in the face of our anger. The issue is not whether we express or do not express our anger. The real issue is *how* we choose to express our experience of anger, *how* we choose to share our anger with others.

Healthy expressions of anger involve two processes: first, the gathering and focusing in upon our anger; and second, the disposing and the removing of the waste and the garbage resulting from that anger. Our modern toilet is an excellent image of these two processes. The toilet bowl collects the waste, and the lever when pressed flushes away the waste. Some of us refuse to focus in upon our anger. Others of us refuse to let go of, to dispose of the anger. We can become addicted to our accumulation of angry, resentful bitter feelings. Each of us has feelings in regard to past helplessness and victimhood that we need to name and claim, and then eliminate. We need to press the lever! We need to flush the toilet!

There are numerous strategies available to us for naming and claiming and disposing of our feelings of anger. These are some recommendations:

1. List persons, places, and events from our past that will evoke anger in us. With compassion and gentleness we need to embrace these feelings, and allow them to work their way through and out of us.

2. Allow an image of how we felt in the past wounding event to surface. We need to remain present to the image and enter into dialogue with it. Summon it to speak with us.

3. Share our expressions of anger with others in the first person — *I*. *I* am resentful; *I* am frustrated; *I* am hostile.

4. Engage in frequent physical exercise. This is important in order to drain off the psychological and muscular tension which anger engenders in us.

Both the Hebrew and the Christian Scriptures provide us with many instances of holy women and men experiencing and expressing anger in an adult, mature manner. Especially do we see the psalmist expressing his anger to Yahweh with child-like candor and simplicity. The psalmist both expresses his anger and his hostile feelings to Yahweh and entrusts to Yahweh the responsibility for bringing about justice, peace, and harmony. Then, freed of his feelings of anger and of his own need to retaliate, the psalmist can move on into his future, unencumbered with his anger, his garbage, his negative feelings and emotions. Both Jesus and Mary present us with instances wherein they experienced and expressed their anger, their resentment with adult freedom and responsibility. Their expressions of anger were assertive, not aggressive.

Adult, mature Christian women and men are called upon at times to experience and to express Christian indignation, a Gospel prophetic posture and stance. We are called to speak up and take action when the God-given dignity of others is negated and ignored. We are called to redress the wrongs and indignities which social and national groups inflict upon the weak, the poor, the minorities, and others who are different. Without such actions of justice, our charity is only a sham, a gesture of condescension, an ego-serving action. We need to express Christian indignation, with righteous anger and courage, wherever we find the dignity of others threatened. We must fearlessly stand up for unity within diversity and reconciliation among peoples who may be in conflict.

FIVE

Anger — Its Many Faces And Expressions

INTRODUCTION

BURIED, PAST ANGER can be easy to discern and to detect in its diverse and varied manifestations if we are attentive observers. Its energies direct and influence our actions and behavior in not-so-subtle ways. These can be directed toward ourselves, toward others, and toward our *Abba*-God. In many instances we are consciously aware that we are angry, that we are being moved and propelled by the energy of buried, past, anger. In this chapter we will consider some of the more obvious and frequent manifestations of our anger-influenced and anger-controlled behavior. We will consider the many faces and expressions which serve as masks and veils for the anger within us which we have not dealt with adequately.

DEPRESSION

MOST OF US at some time in our lives experience periods of depression. Our experience of depression distances, separates, and disengages us from others. We feel walled off from others and enclosed within our own barricades of pain and isolation. We are held hostage within ourselves. For some of us our depression is located in bio-chemical deficiencies which can be addressed in and through chemotherapy. Psychiatry has made tremendous strides in this area through more and more sophisticated use of pharmacological aids. The focus of my attention on depression in this chapter is not directed toward the depression reactions and experiences which are the result of biochemical causes. I am primarily addressing depressive experiences which are behaviorally induced and sustained. Many of us influence the onset of depression through our negligence in attending to our need to name and claim our experience of anger and our need to express in a humane, adult manner our feelings of anger and resentment. Such behaviorally-induced depression is anger turned *inward* upon ourselves. For many of us, our periods of depression are the consequences of our personal dishonesty. We have not lived with the truth of our experience; we have neither claimed how we really felt, nor have we expressed to ourselves and to others our experience of anger, resentment and frustration. In these single instances, or in longer periods of depression, we need to review and to search out any hidden, ignored or denied feelings of anger.

When we experience depression, we need to focus clearly on our genuine inner experience and awareness. We will probably find such times of depression to be marked by feelings of inadequacy, self-accusation and self-blame. Frequently, there are self-punitive elements associated with our depression. Self-demeaning or self-punitive behavior, when present along with a sense of depression, distinguishes it from a normal experience of sadness over a loss. The depression which accompanies a loss — in which we have encountered anger and have also dealt adequately with it — does not usually include self-punitive and masochistic elements. Such experiences of grief and loss are primarily experiences of pain, of woundedness and of profound hurt. They are real, intense experiences of searing suffering. They are not, however compounded and contaminated by anger and retaliatory tendencies.

Jesus knew suffering; Jesus encountered pain in his life, yet we do not have evidence that his suffering was characterized by self-punitive and self-punishing activities. For many of us, though, the time of depression does contain self-punitive and self-retaliative elements. Often our unmerited and unhealthy guilt feelings are part of our experience of depression. Our feelings of guilt are our way of punishing ourselves for failing by not living up to our own expectations or the expectations of others. We lose our self-esteem, our sense of being worthwhile, and our sense of self-respect. And we indulge in condemnation and rejection of ourselves. Usually we surrender the power to be the executives of our lives; instead, we become the executioners of our lives. We do not perceive ourselves as capable of being responsible for supplying our personal needs for life-delight, joy, and pleasure. As hostages within our own prison, we do not see how we can rescue ourselves from our detention and from the onslaughts of our own inner hostility.

The major call which we receive during our experience of depression is the call to change. Our depression is a signal to us that we need to alter something in our life context and situation. We are being summoned to decision. The word *de-cision*, to cut off from, indicates the type of action needed in our life situation. We have to change, re-direct, and re-focus some specific dimension of our lives. Both "No" and "Yes" need to be decisively and actively expressed. The call to change our posture toward a person, place, or situation in our lives involves saying "No" to old ways of relating to them or it. This call to change also involves our saying "Yes" to new ways of relating to a person, place or situation in our lives. This invitation to a risk-filled new way of being challenges us to be both courageous and trusting in our behavior. So it is that our periods of depression contain within them the seeds of change and the call for decisive action. Our old ways of being and doing are not working for us; they are working against us. Choice and decision are paramount! Yes, the call in Deuteronomy 30:11-15, 19 is *our* call during such periods and times of depression:

> For this command which I enjoin on you today
>   is not too mysterious and remote for you.
> It is not up in the sky . . .
> Nor is it across the sea . . .
> No, it is something very close to you,
>   already in your mouths, and in your hearts;
> You have only to carry it out. . . .
> I have today set before you life and prosperity,
>   death and doom. . . .
> I call heaven and earth today
>   to witness against you:
> I have set before you life and death,
>   the blessing and the curse.
> Choose life, then, that you and your descendants may live . . .

As mature adult Christians we struggle to answer the call for change and for the need to make decisions which our times of depression indicate to us as important for our future. Moreover, women tend to be more prone to periods of depression than men are. Yet each of us, female or male, can identify periods of depression in our lives. At such times we were in the trough of the wave, and this position can be painful with its accompanying feelings of helplessness and hopelessness. We have to decide to ride the on-coming wave; we must once again courageously choose life with all its risks and urgent demands upon us.

PASSIVE AGGRESSION

ANOTHER FACE AND EXPRESSION of repressed and inadequately handled anger in our lives is passive-aggressive behavior. Passive-aggressive behavior is characterized by *withholding* ourselves now from persons, places, and events to which we have in the past committed ourselves. People, situations, and social endeavors are left hanging, unattended, and in the lurch with no advance warning of our change of mind, our change of heart. We delay and postpone dealing with important issues, and we put off making decisions which affect our lives as well as the lives of others. We retaliate and punish both ourselves and others in and through the withholding of our time and our energy in a specific endeavor. When we are passive-aggressive we withhold our communication and our participation from people who have a right to expect our direct sharing and our active involvement in their lives or in a given project or endeavor. Passive-aggressive behavior is the most difficult to confront and to deal with effectively. When we are behaving in a passive-aggressive manner we cannot be accused of actively *doing* anything wrong or untoward in relation to anyone. The buried, past unresolved anger that lurks behind our passive aggression asserts itself by what we do *not* say, what we do *not* do. Our negative thrust, our sin, is that of omission rather than commission. When we were young, most of our misdemeanors encompassed those things which we *did*; adult misdemeanors usually involve things which we do *not* do. We refuse to communicate where communication is realistically expected from us, and we refuse to participate actively when involvement is also realistically needed from us. In passive-aggressive behavior we deny our involvement with and our commitment to others. Passive-aggressive behavior is our way of getting even with others; it is also our way of retaliating in a "safe" manner. No one can accuse us of doing anything rude or hurtful. We can hide behind our rationalizations of correct, prudent behavior. Central to passive-aggressive behavior is the inner conflict we experience in relation to our independence from and our dependence upon others. We may even enjoy wounding and hurting others by our lack of participation. They can be stung and annoyed when we refuse to talk about an issue, or when we walk away from persons who need and want to hear our input and our sharing.

Each of us knows of painful times in an open meeting, whether a family discussion or a group gathered together around a given issue or problem, when others who felt strongly about the particular issue and verbalized their feelings and opinions outside the meeting, remained mute and silent within the meeting when the issue was being addressed. Perhaps we ourselves were the ones who remained silent and disengaged during the meeting, and we excused our silence and our muteness. We tend to rationalize our behavior. Underneath much passive-aggressive conduct is the conflict between our posture toward authority and submission. We are struggling with our need to belong and also our need to be independent. We are afraid of being overcome by our own dependency, and we tend to over-react in terms of our independence. When we engage in passive-aggressive behavior, we are functioning as enemies toward others who have reason to believe and to expect that we are their friends and comrades. Our buried, past anger builds walls behind which we hide and remain silent. Our buried, past anger binds and shackles us from reaching out toward others in candid and vulnerable exchanges of opinions and viewpoints. We retreat; we withhold; we distance and barricade ourselves within our own iron cocoons which also deaden and isolate us. Our silence speaks louder than our words; the message is that our best offense is a strong defense.

Many of us who are locked into such passive-aggressive behavior can become addicted to drugs, alcohol, food, nicotine, or work. These provide us with a way of escaping any active participation and involvement with others or with projects that are indigenous to our style of life and our life commitments. We receive satisfaction and respite in and through these addictions. We withdraw from legitimate relationships and social interactions and reach out dependently to crutches of one kind or another. Our addictions provide us with the buffers and the barricades that we want in order to establish and to maintain our distance and disengagement from ourselves and from others. These addictions function as our foxholes shielding us from the fray. We transfer our dependency needs, our need to belong, from legitimate others to objects and behavior which, to our detriment and to our harm, in turn enslave us.

Mature adult Christian women and men realize that both autonomy and submission are part of life. Each of us has to struggle with both our dependency needs and our independence demands. This is not an either-or issue, either dependence or independence. It is a both-and issue, both dependence and independence. Personal choice here is again important. Self-assertive behavior instead of passive-aggressive behavior is needed to help resolve the conflict. There are numerous assertiveness-training programs and also an extensive amount of reading material with which we can become familiar in order to learn the new skills we need to function well.

JEALOUSY, ENVY, AND RESENTMENT

A UNIVERSAL EXPERIENCE which each of us suffers at times is that of jealousy, envy, or resentment. I employ the verb "suffer" advisedly because it is a painful and uncomfortable experience. Jealousy, envy, and resentment are the disturbing feelings which we have at times when we perceive others as superior to us insofar as they have gifts of personality, possessions, status, opportunity, or recognition which we desire. We crave and covet the human qualities, achievements, and possessions which other people enjoy. We perceive our lack of these gifts as reducing us to an inferior position or status. If we had what they have and what we also crave, we would be just as worthwhile as those "lucky ones." Our posture and our attitude toward ourselves is one of inferiority, and our posture and our attitude toward these others is one of jealousy, envy, or resentment. We resent our inferiority and their superiority. The green-eyed monster has us in its grasp! We are again involved in an experience of anger whenever we are caught in the grip of jealousy, envy, or resentment. Underneath such feelings is a painful awareness that we are deprived, squeezed out, and ignored in a given situation. Others have and enjoy what we would like to have and what we really desire. The depth of our resentment can surface such unrealistic perceptions and feelings within us that we begin to resent others not only for having what we covet or lust after, but also for enjoying what should be ours, what really is owed to us and belongs to us. Others are not only enjoying a place in the sun, but they are usurping *our* place in the sun!

Last summer in July a close friend of mine planned to go on vacation to a location in the West that I would have truly enjoyed visiting. I really wanted to go to the mountains in the West. Yet my ministerial commitments during July made it impossible for me to take the time off in order to go with her. My schedule would not allow me any free time until the middle of August. How I envied her! However, it was not a debilitating jealousy for me. I had come to terms with my own time schedule realistically and honestly. Both the time and the place of my vacation would be different. I experienced only an awareness of mild jealousy and envy. For a few days I resented the time flow of my own schedule, which I myself had planned and set. However, through it all, I was able to take delight in the fact that *she* was excited about and looking forward to her trip to the West. And I was able to extend to her good wishes for both a safe journey and an enjoyable rest and relaxation time. My jealousy, envy, and resentment had not reached the point where I resented her going away. There have been times when my own anger-related jealousy, envy, or resentment were strong enough within me to enable me to wish someone both failure and misery. At such times the green-eyed monster really had me by the throat. Moreover, I wanted others to be as miserable and unhappy as I was.

Deprivation, whether real or imagined, is underneath much of the pain and suffering which jealousy, envy, and resentment bring upon us. We experience ourselves as deprived in a given situation. Others are receiving what we need, what we want, and even more what we have a right to; and we are helpless to redress or do anything about our deprived state. Literally, we perceive ourselves as "Poor me!" Buried past anger stirs up these feelings and experiences. Early childhood experiences of physical or psychological deprivation can surface and fuel later feelings of jealousy, envy, or resentment. Some of us adults still function within childish, mythical norms regarding deprivation in relation to differences, to quantity, and to justice. Differences are only differences, yet many of us base our feelings of acceptance and rejection upon differences. Each of us possesses a different need for food — both in kind and in quantity. Our nutritional needs are different, neither inferior nor superior — only different! Some of us require more time for rest, for leisure, for work, for socializing, for physical exercise. Temperament, personality, and style of life demand different expenditures of time and energy from us. Again, these are only differences! We adults seem to have a difficult time converting to adult norms relating to needs and wants which encourage difference among us. Our "Keeping-up-with-the-Joneses" mentality results from both childish and wishful thinking.

We women religious have had to struggle with this issue because so much of our lives within community in the past stressed uniformity and conformity. One of the women religious I work with shared an experience related to the issue of difference with me. Sister Ellen approached her major superior to ask for the permission and the funds to accompany another sister to Germany. The major superior was stunned. Yet the communications from the congregation had been stressing that the sisters turn in their gift money to the congregation and ask for congregational funds for their travel. These messages were encouraging the sisters not to use private gift money for foreign travel. The major superior, who did not understand differing needs answered, "Well, Ellen, if I give you the money, then I have to release money for trips to *all* of the sisters." Sister Ellen's immediate response spontaneously burst forth from her, "Sister, that's ridiculous! Over one-half of the sisters don't have any desire to cross an ocean. Another one-fourth of them are too infirm to travel. And of the remaining one-fourth, the majority of them would not be free to leave their apostolic commitments. So you have about fifteen sisters who could approach you for money for a trip abroad. The vast majority of these fifteen sisters do not want to go to Europe now or are unable to plan now for foreign travel." The major superior recognized the realism of the situation and agreed with Sister Ellen's assessment. Sister Ellen received both the permission and the funds for the trip to Germany. Central to this discussion were the issues of difference and uniformity. If one sister were to gain the permission and the funds for travel, then each of the sisters would have to go to Europe. On the other hand, personal needs and wants differ among us. We have different needs and different wants. We do not usually need or want what another person needs and wants. Each family, each group has to negotiate this issue in terms of individual needs and wants. Each of us has to take the responsibility for *asking for what we need and want*. Chances are that when we receive what we need and want we will enjoy peace and security and not be as strongly prone to feelings of jealousy, envy, and resentment. It is our responsibility to inform others of our needs and wants. They cannot be expected to guess and to anticipate our needs the way our parents did when we were still in diapers. Jesus addressed this issue when he told us to ask for what we need, to seek out what we wanted, and to knock on a closed door. He directed us to take hold of our responsibility for asking, seeking, and knocking on the door with trust, simplicity, and candor.

Justice is the virtue which directs equitable distribution of goods and resources to others. The quality of equity relates to our needs and our wants; equity is not primarily concerned with equal and exact measurement of the quantity of one's giving and receiving. Some of us tend to confuse equality and equity. We want an equal (exact measurement in terms of quantity) piece of the pie, rather than the amount required or needed by the person eating the pie. (The size of the pie and the number of people expecting a piece of the pie is another issue). As adults our needs and wants determine our choices and our decisions. However, when we were younger, many of the decisions made for us were based upon the criterion of need. As we grow older and we mature, the quality of our adult lives depends not only upon our needs for survival, but also upon our adult wants which expand and change with maturity. The fulfillment of our adult needs and wants satiate the hunger of our spirit-life which cannot be denied by us or others without narrowing and constricting our personality. Older people have different yet compelling spirit-life wants which cluster around experiences of both beauty and leisure. Older women and men dream dreams, and their dreams call us to listen and attend to them.

SARCASM AND DARK HUMOR

ANOTHER VERY LETHAL WEAPON which buried, past anger employs very skillfully is the poisoned tongue. Our sarcastic speech unsheaths and reveals both to us and to others how deep and how buried are our past experiences of anger. Some of us are bitterly critical, cruel, and wounding with others in the name of possessing a quick wit or a clever turn of a word or phrase. Sarcasm is a cowardly hit-and-run device. We cut the person down with a caustic remark, and then we escape and take refuge while the person endeavors to recover. We are engaging in guerrilla warfare. And people around us are afraid of our verbal abuse. We ourselves are also helpless in the face of another's sarcasm. It is levelled at us so ruthlessly and so unexpectedly that we are rendered speechless. Humor can also be employed as a weapon. Some of us need an object of derision, of ridicule, or of scorn in order to perceive ourselves and have others perceive us as witty or humorous. Such humor is active-aggressive humor. A group can be enjoying our penetrating humor while the wounded person bleeds within herself/himself. Another image which expresses the devastating power of dark humor is acid. Buried, past anger emerges and poisons our humor with its acid. The dark, anger-provoked humor of some of us can be likened to an intravenous acid-drip constantly flowing drop-by-drop into the blood stream of others. We burn and sear others through our negative darts. Our dark humor is an act of violence; it wounds, dissolves, and corrodes any inclusive or cooperative response from others. Such humor keeps others at a distance and keeps them on the defensive in relation to us, and gradually such humor destroys any possibility of establishing humane, Christ-like trust among us.

HURT, FORGIVENESS, AND RECONCILIATION

DORIS DONNELLY indicates that there are three steps or stages in the journey from hurt to reconciliation: hurt, forgiveness, and then reconciliation (*Learning to Forgive* and *Putting Forgiveness into Practice*). Our hurt is the conflict, hate, anger, misery, or discomfort which we are experiencing in relation to another's indifference, cruelty, meanness, injustice or arrogance toward us. The subjective element in feelings and emotions is important in terms of hurt and anger. The depth of the hurt and anger does not depend upon how much or how little was said or done to us. For most of us the degree to which we become hurt, angry, or hostile is related to our own expectations. For some of us our expectations regarding how we are to be treated, how we are to be responded to, and how people we really care for are to relate to us are shattered and broken. We expected agreement, understanding, and trust in a given situation. We depended upon it and assumed these sentiments were there. They were not. How devastating! Donnelly cautions us to give sufficient attention to our need for entering into the process of forgiveness.

When we are wounded by broken expectations and in pain, it takes time to heal and it takes time to forgive. Forgiveness — giving for another's future — is the theme Jesus spoke of most frequently. Over and over in the Gospel we see and we hear "You are forgiven" and "Forgive others." Many of us confuse reconciliation with the painful and time-consuming process of forgiveness. Forgiveness is the process wherein we cleanse the laceration, dress and drain the wound, withdraw from full participation in our regular activities during this time of healing. During all of the time of healing there is much pain, suffering, and discomfort. The major struggle during our healing or forgiveness period is the desire for revenge or retaliation. Tending to our wounds brings its own pain, and the temptation to react toward ourselves and others with even more violence and injustice can be quite enticing for us. Yet the Gospel calls us to a non-violent, a life-giving, and a non-resistance posture — *forgiveness*! Jesus' invitation to forgive is not mere empty speech. He experienced hurt, hostility, and injustice. He distanced himself for the time he needed for prayer and for healing. He forgave. He also reached out with forgiveness to others. Donnelly presents these characteristics of the forgiveness of Jesus:

1. Jesus initiates forgiveness. The person does not approach *him* and ask for forgiveness. Jesus reaches out and initiates forgiveness. He begins it.

2. Jesus confers self-worth and self-esteem upon the person whom he forgives. Jesus called Peter to be the leader of his small band of disciples, even though Peter had denied him. For Jesus, to forgive is to extend trust and confidence in the person. Also in the parable of the Prodigal Son, the father who loves unconditionally bestows numerous gifts on his son

who is contrite and remorseful: an affectionate embrace, jewelry, a new wardrobe, sandals, and a party with his friends to welcome and to celebrate his return home — reconciliation.

3. Jesus does not let hurt stand in the way of the relationship. He reaches out to both Judas and Peter, even though each has betrayed him. In the hurt and woundedness, Jesus continues to love and to reach out to others who have failed in their relationship with *Abba*-God and others.

4. Jesus cancels the debt of guilt when he forgives. The slate is wiped clean, and nothing is owed to him. Jesus does not put a price on his forgiveness. Forgiveness is sheer gift!

Furthermore, Donnelly describes reconciliation as the process which brings together that which belongs together, but which is apart. The coming together which reconciliation implies can occur only when there has been sufficient distance for healing and for the restoration of personal well-being. Many of us endeavor to precipitate reconciliation before personal well-being and healing have taken place. We cannot move toward and reach out to another in reconciliation when we are still maimed and in need of more recuperative time. The nature of our relationship also demands to be reviewed. Some of us do not "belong" together; without radical changes of personality and priorities, some relationships will continue to be destructive, violent, and devastating for us.

For further understanding and illumination of the destructive consequences of buried past anger, the books and tapes of Dennis and Matthew Linn would be of great help to many of us. They address the healing of memories — the healing of past wounds and hurts which still affect and influence our present lives and in many ways prevent us from entering fully and freely into our future. Their books focus upon the process of forgiveness: *Healing of Memories and Healing Life's Hurts.*

Christian reconciliation asserts that basically we are one; it acknowledges that fundamentally, in our spirit-life, we are daughters and sons of *Abba*-God and sisters and brothers of one another in Christ Jesus. In Christian faith we name and claim the reality that we are needy, that we are incomplete, that we are vulnerable human beings. From ourselves we need gentleness, tenderness, challenge, praise, protection, comfort, mercy, and forgiveness. From others we need recognition, encouragement, challenge, companionship, inclusion, and the sharing of time and interests. To others we also owe recognition, the sharing of interests, time, and energy, encouragement, challenge, companionship, comfort, and inclusion. I remember the words of an aged, wise priest who said, "To *Abba*-God we owe obedience and listening; to others we owe mercy and compassion."

SUMMARY

BURIED, PAST ANGER stirs up and fuels our anger-controlled behavior, a reaction of which many of us are not consciously aware because we do not realize that our actions are influenced by old anger and resentment. Anger-influenced behavior has many faces and expressions which mask and hide the rage still buried within us. Some of these expressions of buried and denied anger are:

1. *Depression.* Behaviorally-induced depression is anger turned *inward* upon ourselves. Our depressive periods indicate to us that we have not faced up to the truth of our

experience; we have neither claimed how we feel, nor have we expressed to ourselves and to others our experience of anger, resentment, or frustration. Usually there are self-punitive and self-retaliative elements in our depression. We lose our self-esteem, our sense of being worthwhile, and our self-respect. The major call which we receive through our experience of depression is the call to change, the call to decision and choice. Old ways of being and doing are not working for us; they are working against us. Choice and decision are important!

2. *Passive-Aggression.* When we are passive-aggressive we withhold our communication and our participation from people who have a right to expect our direct sharing and our active involvement in their lives or in a given project or endeavor. The buried, past unresolved anger within us asserts itself by what we do *not* say, what we do *not* do. Central to passive-aggressive behavior is the inner conflict we experience in relation to our independence from and our dependence upon others. We struggle both with our need to belong and our need to be independent. Self-assertive behavior, instead of passive-aggressive behavior, is needed to enable us to resolve the conflict.

3. *Jealousy, Envy and Resentment.* These are the feelings which we experience when we both crave and covet the human qualities, achievements, and possessions which other people have. Others have and enjoy what we would like to have and what we really desire; in some instances we even resent others for enjoying what should be ours, what really is owed to us and belongs to us. Deprivation, either real or imagined, is underneath much of the pain and suffering which jealousy, envy and resentment inflict upon us. Some of us have to re-examine our attitude toward difference. Differences are only differences unless we bestow upon them judgments of superiority or inferiority. We have differing needs

and wants, and these determine to a large degree our adult choices and decisions. Uniformity and conformity are childish norms which at times influence our adult judgments and behavior.

4. *Sarcasm and Dark Humor.* Our sarcastic speech reveals both to us and to others how deeply buried are our past experiences of anger. Sarcasm is a cowardly hit-and-run device. We can be bitterly critical, cruel and hurtful toward others in the name of possessing a quick wit or the gift of a sharp one-line retort. Humor can also be employed as a weapon. Some of us need an object of derision, of ridicule, and of scorn in order to perceive and have others perceive us as witty or humorous. Such humor is active-aggressive humor and manages to keep others at a distance and on the defensive in relation to us.

In whatever way our buried, past anger asserts itself in our behavior and in our relationships, its manifestation calls us to attend to the wounding in our past which has not healed. Doris Donnelly stresses, both in her writing and in her lectures, our need for healing before we can forgive and be reconciled. Healing takes time and is painful. Some of us deny the depth of hurt and pain which situations in our past inflicted upon us. These wounds have to be attended to, have to be dressed, and have to receive the time, the distance, and the rest which they need for healing. Only after some healing occurs, are we ready for forgiveness and ready to forgive. Forgiveness and then reconciliation cannot be imposed and forced upon us.

Jesus is unique in history insofar as he stresses our *need* to forgive and to be forgiven. Forgiveness is the issue which Jesus emphasized most strongly in his outreach to others, in his teachings, and in his parables. Forgiveness — mercy and compassion — are the genuine signs of Christian love and Christian charity in mature adult Christian women and men.

SIX

Fear — Healthy And Unhealthy

INTRODUCTION

FEAR IS AN EXPERIENCE which each of us has to confront, both in terms of its influence in our past, and even now in terms of its influence in our present life situation. We are not strangers to the experience of fear. Our childhood had a strong influence upon our initiation into fear. Early childhood is the time for dragons, monsters, and scary creatures which we imagined to be in the dark, under the bed, in the closet, in the basement, and also in our dreams. Childhood is a time for magic and fantasy — a time for ghosts and goblins. Perhaps some of us even had a haunted house in our neighborhood which further stimulated our fantasy and our sense of magic. During early childhood a child's fantasy life and sense of magic is not yet rooted in reality. A youngster does not have enough data and information or sufficient reasoning power to root her/his magical perceptions within reality. So it is then that a child's fantasy and sense of magic functions unchecked and in disregard of logical thinking. Moreover, reality testing is difficult for young children. Even as adults we often have to check some of our perceptions with reality. "Where did I hear that? Did I dream this?" is a frequent process that we employ to distinguish fantasy and magical thinking from reality.

Each of us has a residue of these early childhood phantoms and phantasms in us which are distortions of reality. The dark, along with certain other images and things, frighten us even now. Some of these things are roaches, rats, snakes, dogs, cats, lightning or thunderstorms. Each of us also possesses a reservoir of scary, traumatic, or frightening experiences which are part of our own personal history. Six years ago I lived with two Dominican Sisters. One was phobic regarding roaches (they are plentiful in New Orleans) and the other Sister enjoyed a phobia regarding mice. For two years I dealt with all of the roach and mice problems — dead or alive — in the house. In early childhood we may have experienced some frightening events which terrorize us still. Moreover, early in childhood some of us have witnessed scenes or events in our homes of physical violence from alcoholic or abusive parents, or we may have been abandoned or lost. We may have suffered the loss of a parent through death or prolonged separation. Some of us may have undergone physical injury, illness, or a crippling accident whereas others may have suffered from insecurity, physical abuse, the loud verbal noises of disagreement and fighting, or even violence to ourselves or our surroundings.

OUR EXPERIENCE OF FEAR

FEAR IS A FEELING OR EMOTION which we experience when we are aware of or when we anticipate crisis, danger, or evil. These feelings are also accompanied by physiological responses — increase of heartbeat, sweating palms, shortness of breath, coldness in our hands and feet, and other symptoms. During periods of fear large quantities of adrenalin are secreted. The human organism readies itself for action. However, this physiological readiness can overmobilize the person in instances of panic, and terror-ridden behavior can become disorganized, confused, and without focus. Some of us who experience frequent fear and prolonged states of arousal may suffer psychosomatic disorders as a result of continual stress and drain on the body's systems. Central to the consideration of fear is the rootedness of our fear in objective reality. Is the perceived impending crisis, danger, or evil real? Or is our fear rooted in fantasy or magical thinking? The power of our imagination has a tremendous capacity to create viable solutions and options or to create problems, dangers, and thus more fear. How we choose to activate the creative powers of our imagination determines how successful we will be in leading lives which are not controlled or dominated by fantasy and magical thinking.

The experience of fear in the presence of real crisis, real danger, or real evil is healthy fear; it is an asset. Such experience mobilizes us both physiologically and psychologically to confront or to withdraw from the threatening reality. Such experience can be empowering for us in our encounters with crisis, danger, or evil. On the other hand, experiences of fear or panic rooted in the distortions of fantasy and magical thinking are unhealthy. Such experiences can be continually debilitating and diminishing for us who are frequently in the power and grasp of imagined crisis, danger, or evil. It takes a great amount of creative energy to cope if our lives are continually constricted by the experience of unhealthy fear. Our experience of fear is real, whether we are responding to *real* or *imagined* threats of crisis, danger, or evil. However the question of whether the basis of the fear lies in reality or in fantasy determines whether the fear is healthy or unhealthy. In some situations we experience both healthy and unhealthy fear.

During childhood many of our fears may have centered around such issues as loud or unusual noises, unfamiliar and strange persons and places, or unexpected movements from dogs, cats, or other creeping and crawling things. Later on in childhood, especially during the time of elementary school, fear can be associated with issues of right and wrong, competition, sickness and death, and measuring up to the expectations of parents and teachers. During adolescence a new issue emerges — acceptance from the peer group and the fear of being ridiculed, ignored, or challenged by it . Adulthood with its many responsibilities and privileges surfaces different types of fear within us. We fear death and illness not only in terms of their personal cost to us, but also in terms of the cost and the consequences to those people who depend upon us. We are also moved by fear when we worry about our personal inadequacies in relation to fulfilling our social responsibilities or when we worry about our job security, our health, and our social status. For older adults the fear of not being able to earn a living, of not having enough financial security for the declining years, and of having to endure a lengthy, painful, and helpless terminal illness is quite real. Many of us do not fear death itself so much as we fear a dependent and extended period of time spent in suffering and dying. Other factors which we have to deal with include the cultural influences upon our fear. Our culture gives permission to express fear to females more readily than to males. The macho image cultivated in certain segments of our society makes it unmanly for a male to show or express fear. Women, the "weaker" sex, may more often express fear without shame or censure.

Psychologists indicate that each of us develops our own fear pattern and process which is dependent upon three factors: (1) the behavior of people whom we imitate or with whom we identify; (2) the way in which we have been influenced by people in our childhood; and (3) the traumatic events or experiences which we have had in our lives. So it is that our fear threshold is related to our identifica-

Fear — Healthy and Unhealthy

tion, to our conditioning, or to our trauma early in childhood. In fact, our fear process can be related to a combination of these three factors. I also submit that the unique and singular spirit of our own personhood affects our interaction with the three factors mentioned above. In any case, the message which our fear delivers to us is a message concerning our helplessness, our vulnerability, our inability to cope with given situations. We perceive ourselves as incompetent, ineffective, and hopeless in the crisis, danger, or evil. Our sense of helplessness descends into the despairing stance of *hopelessness*. We are lost.

Our usual response to such dire threats to our personhood can be a "fight-or-flight" response. Our "fight" response makes us protective, aggressive, even hostile to persons and events which signal crisis, danger, or evil to us. "They are out to get me" is the attitude of fear which pervades such relationships with others. Unhealthy fear enables us to imagine that the worst can and will happen; we are disappointed when the worst does not take place; and we are gratified when the worst does occur ("I knew this would happen!"). The expected and programmed worst is grist for the mill of our enemy within — our unhealthy fear-dominated imagination. Our "flight" response is usually one of withdrawal, distancing and disengaging ourselves for the present. It is a passive-dependent response. We clam up; we dig in; we retreat to gather our resources for another encounter at a future time. We hide!

Within the experience of fear from imagined crisis, danger, or evil is an energy-packed and power-packed message we give to ourselves — *"Don't Exist!"* We adults victimize ourselves with this negative message which only serves to reinforce our perception that we are helpless and hopeless; that we are powerless, cursed, puny and weak, a failure and no good. Others and the world are more powerful than we are or ever can be. Poor weak me! This is a very painful and agonizing experience. Our fear reduces us to a position and a posture of *victimhood*. We perceive ourselves as "less than" or "not as good as" others and others are "more than" or "better than" we are. We are too little, and others are too much for us.

In our victimhood posture, we abdicate our personal and individual responsibility for our own lives. Subtly and surely we begin to expect and to demand that family members, colleagues at work, and our friends *take care of us*. We refuse to make our own decisions and choices, we refuse to take responsibility for our lives and to accept the consequences which such responsibility entails. Presently I am working with a middle-aged woman, who is a widow. Both in her early life at home and then later in her marriage, she abdicated from her responsibility for making decisions and choices. Now in her second year of widowhood, she is quite angry with her three children and the government for their "neglect" of her. Financially she is adequately secure, yet she resists making the decisions which could provide her with both personal and economic security in regard to her future. Realistically she needs to sell her family home, buy or rent a smaller house, and continue her relationships with friends she has known through the years. She is still a healthy, vibrant, and active lady. Yet she does not want to assume responsibility for her life; she is indulging herself in her resistance; she is more comfortable enjoying a victim posture towards her life. I had arranged for her to meet with a competent financial advisor, who informed her of her viable financial options. Still she prefers to function as an incompetent woman who wants other people to make her decisions for her. Presently she is struggling with the issue of whether she wants to make her own decisions and choices, that is, whether she chooses to be responsible for her life and for the consequences of her decisions, or not. I think she will assume responsibility; I trust her to do what she has to do.

Fear — Healthy and Unhealthy

Fear is at work in us when we refuse to stir up and to summon forth our inner resources and powers in order to handle well the situations which we meet in our daily living. We succumb to discouragement and perceive ourselves as unable to make certain segments of our lives work effectively for us. For many of us our "I can't" is really "I won't." We refuse to actualize our inner potential and abilities. We negate our power to choose, our ability to create different options and to shape future consequences in our lives. Many of us prefer to utilize stop-gap measures in our daily living rather than to think through and plan what we need to do in order to change unpleasant and unproductive elements in our relationships. As a result, we do not resolve or dissipate the forces of crisis, danger, or evil within our lives. Many of us fear and withdraw from the pain which self-observation and self-examination entail and exact from us. Then our own laziness and sloth keep us imprisoned within our narcissistic illusions regarding ourselves. M. Scott Peck in *People of the Lie* (pp. 69-77) treats this issue of fear with candor and clarity.

Our refusal to stop, to discontinue, and to turn off the wishful thinking which so inflates our unhealthy fear serves only to maintain and magnify our fear responses. We can become locked into a vicious circle in respect to the experience and the expression of fear! In such situations we need to *stop* and *think*. We need to replace our impractical fantasy with cold reality, with facts and concrete information; we need to replace our wishful thinking with logical, reasoned reflection. We need both to gather information and to process it dispassionately. Logical thinking and sound intellectual reasoning shrink the fantasy, diffuse the euphoria of wishful thinking, and bring into realistic focus the unreality which we have been creating in and through our fear. Especially in contemporary society do we need to stop the whirl of our lives and examine frequently where our stress, our anxiety, and our feelings of being trapped and constricted are coming from. The threat of economic insecurity, of nuclear warfare, of crime-related personal injury, of illness and disease are continual sources of fear for many of us. Many of us live our lives under a great burden of realistic stress and pressure. At times we question our capacity to cope, our strength to ward off these dangers, and our ability merely to survive. We need to address our fear, dialogue with our apprehensions, and convert their energies into creative solutions for our lives. Truly fear is an energy, a powerful source of movement and momentum, and yet this force can function as either our friend or as our foe. We cultivate healthy fear as a friend when we are able to be present to this friend, dialogue with this friend, and utilize in a constructive way the resources which this friend shares with us. We confirm unhealthy fear as an enemy when we ignore and deny the reality of its powerful presence, decline to communicate with it and surrender to it — in defeat and despair — our autonomy and our inner resources. The waters of the ocean remind me of fear in relation to our lives. The winds can move the vessels which ride upon the surface of the sea and nurture the marine life deep within the ocean or the winds can stir up the waters to the point of destroying the same sea-going ships and the life within the waters. Maintaining the tension between what is healthy and unhealthy is one of the tasks of our adult lives. How do we deal creatively with the real crises, dangers, or evils in our lives? How do we choose to deal with the imagined crises, dangers, or evils in our lives?

Our own experience of fear usually has its own pattern and rhythm. For some of us our experience of fear peaks in the future, *before* the crisis, the danger, or the evil threatening us is actually upon us. We imagine and fantasize about the threatening events which may take place. We allow our imagination to run the gamut in anticipating all the terrible consequences which can befall us. Usually this experience of anticipatory fear contains both healthy and unhealthy dimensions. We expect the worst. Such fear can immobilize us unless we stop and think; we have to gather information and process the data. Many of the terrifying consequences can be avoided if we strategize well and choose to plan in such a way that the dangers we anticipated can be reduced or eliminated. For some of us our experience of fear peaks in the present, *during* the crisis, the danger, or the evil. We lose heart and become afraid in the midst of dealing with the threatening event. Some of us find it difficult to complete arduous tasks and to follow through during a crisis, because we are overcome with feelings of fear and inadequacy. We are the ones who tend to "jump ship" in times of stress and pressure. For others of us the experience of fear peaks in the past, *after* we have negotiated and struggled through a crisis, a danger, or an evil situation. We are overwhelmed with the fear of our inadequate behavior. We allow guilt to overcome and to torture us. We succumb to guilt-fear experiences when we are aware that we have not performed well, that we have not met our expectations (real or unreal), that we have missed the mark in our behavior in a given situation. We blew it! We are threatened by the wrongdoing, by the inadequacy, or by the evil of our behavior, and we fear we cannot in any way undo or eradicate the consequences of our action. Willard Gaylin in *Feelings* indicates that guilt "is a form of self-disappointment. It is the sense of anguish that we do not achieve our standards of what we ought to be. We have fallen short. We have somehow or other betrayed some internal sense of potential self" (p. 50). Many of us indulge ourselves with the guilt-fear experience of perceiving ourselves as never being able to be forgiven or never being able to be freed of our wrongdoing, of our mistakes, or of our sin; we are not worthy of forgiveness; we are not good enough to be forgiven. In and through guilt we cannot have a future with the promise of peace and joy because of our apprehension and anxiety regarding the merciless predicament of our lives before self, before others, and before our God. We can better deal effectively with our moments of fear when we have an indication of our peak-time pattern regarding our experiences of fear in the face of crisis, danger, or evil.

SACRED SCRIPTURE AND FEAR

THE HUMAN FEELING AND EMOTION which the Scriptures confront and address most frequently is fear — both healthy and unhealthy fear. Both the Hebrew and the Christian Scriptures speak to the fear, the dread, the anxiety, and the apprehension of women and men in their encounters with real and imagined crisis, danger, or evil. Fear is a major theme that moves through all of the Scriptures from Genesis through Revelation. In the Garden of Eden we witness Adam and Eve after the fall hiding from Yahweh and then Adam hiding in guilt-ridden fear behind Eve's leather skirts (Genesis 3:8-12). Early on after Abram's call from Yahweh to leave his family and homeland, we discover that he also experienced fear. The Lord told Abram, "Fear not, Abram! I am your shield; I will make your reward very great" (Genesis 15:1). Moses also became immobilized with fear upon receiving his call and his mission. For me there is a delightfully humorous exchange contained in the dialogue of Moses with the Lord. Moses spent almost twenty-six verses quickly and vehemently protesting his verbal inadequacy to represent the wishes of the Lord to Pharaoh. He resists and insists repeatedly that he is "slow of speech"; in exasperation, the Lord commissions Aaron to be the spokesman (Exodus 3 and 4). Jeremiah, Isaiah, Ezekiel, Amos, and Jonah bear witness to their fear and anxiety in doing what the Lord called each of them to accomplish. Mary herself succumbs to fear upon hearing the initial message that she is favored by God. The angel addressed her fear, calmed her down before communicating to her the basic information concerning her call to be the mother of Jesus. Mary also had to work through her healthy fear and deep apprehension before she was able to surrender freely to God's will (Luke 1:26-38). Mary's struggle with fear has always been a comfort to me as I perceive her be *the* woman of the Gospel; the experience of healthy fear was not foreign to her. The apostles and followers of Jesus had to confront and then handle their fear at given moments in their shared life with Jesus.

One of the basic themes of the Scriptures which precipitates both healthy and unhealthy fear within all of us involves three movements: the Election, the Mission, and the Presence Promise or Blessing. Simply expressed this theme reads, "Go! Do! I-AM-WITH-YOU!" All through the Scriptures women and men are seen struggling painfully with their experience of fear in their encounter with the call of God, with their experience of fear in accepting the mission or work which God summons them to do, and with their experience of fear in embracing the promise that the enabling power and presence of God would be with them in doing God's will. Example upon example parades before us of women and men having to encounter their fear (healthy and unhealthy) when they have been encountered by the Lord and then confronted by his Word. For adult Christians our encounter with the Lord surfaces the deepest of fears within us and the most profound dread of which we are capable. In both the Judaic and the Christian religious traditions we learn that the Lord searches the depths of the human spirit and reaches into the secret recesses of the soul wherein we tend to hide our healthy and unhealthy fear from both ourselves and others. Our God calls us to encounter the fear in our bones and to accept his transforming presence and power to overcome the dark and dread-filled areas of our being. Rudolf Otto writes of the Mystery of the Holy which both frightens and fascinates us when we are grasped by its power and presence. He terms these mysterious moments and movements the *mysterium tremendum* and *mysterium fascinans* (*The Idea of the Holy*, pp. 12-24). At times the *mysterium tremendum*, (the mystery of awesomeness), inspires in us a profound awareness of our creaturehood, our littleness, and our nothingness when we are in the presence of the Wholly Other, the Holy One, the God of Power and Might. A sense of awe and wonder simply overwhelms us. The awesomeness of God is wonder-filled! The Christian liturgy employs a passage from Isaiah which echoes this awareness — we pray, "Holy, holy, holy Lord, God of power and might, heaven and earth are full of your glory."

Jesus was well aware of the well-springs of healthy and unhealthy fear deeply buried within our human personhood. He knew and understood both healthy and unhealthy fear. Moreover, he also knew the danger which we encounter in unrealistic, magical thinking, and fantasy-produced fear. "Fear not!" "Do not be anxious!" and "Do not be afraid!" were his frequently reiterated responses to women and men who were crippled by their fear. Such messages of encouragement were the most frequent communication he shared with others in his relationship with them. The Gospels contain over sixty such sayings of encouragement and trust to others in their experience of fear — both healthy and unhealthy. Jesus struggled with his own healthy fear during significant and threatening events in his own life and also encouraged his

Fear — Healthy and Unhealthy

followers to confront their fear. He went even further. He promised to be with them (and with us) in the ongoing struggle with fear. "Go! Do! I-am-*with*-you!" confronts and consoles us today as we wrestle with our fear, both healthy and unhealthy.

The Election, the Mission, and Promise of his Presence or Blessing were also strongly active in the life and message of Jesus. He promised not to leave his followers and his friends orphans; he would send his Spirit and this he did. Pentecost empowered the followers and the friends of Jesus with both hope and courage. Christian women and men through the centuries have affirmed their empowerment in and through the gift of the Spirit in their lives. It is the Spirit, our Comforter and our Consoler, who is *with* us in multiple crises, dangers, and evil situations which we encounter in the course of our lives. One of the special gifts and powers which the Spirit shares with us is *hope*. This gift enables us to move into the future with an awareness that the choices we make will make a difference in our own lives and in the lives of others. Hope enables our future, our tomorrow, to be viable and possible. Hope enables us to trust that our inner resources will be effective in dealing with the day-to-day situation. Hope enables us to expect both the presence and power of the Spirit to energize the movement and happenings of tomorrow. Hope enables us to expect that with the Spirit's presence and power in our life situations we are capable of dealing well with our lives and are able to trust the surprises that emerge within them. Hope enables us to say the "Yes" and the "No" that each choice-eliciting event calls forth from us. Hope reaches out to grasp the extended and helping hand of God in accomplishing the next task. Hope brings us the assurance that the Spirit of God is with us no matter what. Hope assures us that we are loved by God, empowered by God, and forgiven by

God. Hope reminds us that the Father of Christ Jesus and our *Abba*-God is a God of mercy, compassion, and unconditional love. Hope enables us to dismiss and to cast away any unhealthy fear of God's condemnation, of God's abandonment of us, of God's cruel negation or rejection of us. Hope enables us to trust the loving-kindness of *Abba*-God again, and again, and again. Hope energizes and empowers us. Hope is sheer gift of God to us!

Another gift of the Spirit which adult Christian women and men enjoy is the gift of *courage*. Courage is heart-power; courage is core-self power; courage is soul-power. Courage enables us to act and to function from the depths of the divine power and presence within us. Courage enables us to call forth and to stir up from within us the very power of the Risen Christ in our encounters with crisis and danger. With courage we sound the secret depths of our being and bring to the surface unknown strength and ability to be and to do what is needed in given situations. We all can acknowledge moments of courage, moments which were of short duration and also lengthy periods of endurance under very difficult and stressful circumstances. We also can acknowledge moments of dis-couragement, moments when we lost heart, when we lost our sense of purpose and meaning, when we surrendered to fear and assumed that we were lost. En-couragement was the gift we received during our period of discouragement. The Spirit of the Risen Christ gives encouragement. Others who are Spirit-filled and Spirit-led also are tremendous sources of encouragement for us. The Spirit ministers to us in and through them. Encouragement enables us to become centered again in terms of both the power and presence of the Spirit within us, within others, and of course within the situations in our lives. The Spirit through encouragement enables us to remember who we are and who *Abba*-God is in relation to us. We are his beloved children; he is our nurturing and protecting (parenting) God. Encouragement enables us to love in peace and joy and with patience and perseverance. Such encouragement is not merely ego-stroking activity. It is the assurance that within ourselves we have the presence and the power to be and to do what *Abba*-God wants from us and for us; we have the power to achieve our wellbeing. Courage enables us to claim the Spirit as our Comforter — she who brings strength and vigor (*fortitudo* = strength) when we experience ourselves as weak and wan. Courage enables us also to claim the Spirit as Consoler — she who is with us when we are alone and unattended (*solitudo* = alone). She is with us in moments of painful solitude and situations wherein we have to do-it-alone. In our solo moments which threaten and frighten us she is with us. She is there. Courage energizes us and empowers us from within the deep recesses of our personhood. Courage is a remarkable gift to us from God. We rejoice! We relax! The Spirit is with us!

As mature, adult Christian women and men frequently we need to review, in and through prayer, the issues of fear buried deep inside us. Frequent prayer is a means through which we can come into contact with our hidden healthy and unhealthy fear. Reflective prayer enables us to encounter the truth of who we are and the truth of who we are not. For many of us it is quite helpful to select a passage from Scripture which contains an issue of fear. We can identify with the woman or the man who in the chosen passage was experiencing fear, even the specific issue of our own fear, and bring the fear to the Lord. The Spirit within us enables us to name and claim the fear and also enables us to embrace the energies of hope and courage which we need to confront and to shrink the power of the fear. The hidden fear within us needs to be encountered and then transformed by the inner energies and graces which are also within us. This process is a deep-unto-deep process, a Spirit-unto-spirit process. It enables us to stir up the dormant energies, graces, and powers we all possess. Through reflective prayer we come into contact with our Spirit-self, our true self, the truth of ourselves. We also need numerous Pentecosts — we need to experience the presence of God and to receive from him the strength and power to manage our lives with truth and charity. Through frequent reflective prayer we surface our unhealthy fear especially in regard to our relationship with *Abba*-God. Many of us still harbor deep fear which is more the result of our childish religious fantasy and our brooding. For many of us our God is still the God of lightning and thunder, the cruel God of doom and damnation. We still perceive ourselves as unworthy of God's love, unworthy of compassion and forgiveness. Many of us are still with Moses on Mount Sinai instead of with Jesus on the Mount of the Beatitudes. Our God is severe, unforgiving, and sadistic. We have yet to encounter the Good Shepherd, the *Abba*-God who searches with care and concern for the lost and wounded lamb. Frequent reflective prayer and meditation enable us to put on the mind and heart of Christ Jesus in relating to *Abba*-God, to ourselves, and to others.

SUMMARY

WE ARE NO STRANGERS to the experience of fear. Our childhood is the time of magic and fantasy. During early childhood a child's fantasy life and sense of magic are not yet rooted in reality. Each of us also possesses a reservoir of scary, traumatic, or frightening experiences which are part of our own personal history. Fear is a feeling or emotion which we experience when we are aware of or when we anticipate crisis, danger, or evil. These feelings and awarenesses of fear are also accompanied by physiological responses. Central to the consideration of fear is the rootedness of our fear in objective reality. Healthy fear is rooted in real crisis, real danger, or real evil. Unhealthy fear is rooted in the crisis, danger, or evil which our fantasy or magical thinking creates and projects. Psychologists indicate that each of us develops our own fear pattern and process which is dependent upon three factors: (1) the behavior of people whom we imitate or with whom we identify; (2) the way in which we have been influenced by people in our childhood; and (3) the traumatic events or experiences which we have had in our lives.

The message which our fear delivers to us is a message concerning our helplessness, our vulnerability, our inability to cope with given situations. We perceive ourselves as incompetent, ineffective, and hopeless in the crisis, danger, or evil. Our usual response to such threats to our personhood is the "fight-or-flight" response. Our "fight" response makes us very aggressive, even hostile, to persons and events which signal crisis, danger, or evil to us. Our "flight" response is usually one of withdrawal, distancing and dis-engagement. Fear, especially unhealthy fear, places us in the posture of "victim" in which we abdicate our personal and individual responsibility for our own lives. We begin to expect and to demand that family members, colleagues at work, and our friends take care of us. We refuse to make our own decisions and choices; we refuse to take responsibility for our lives and to accept the consequences which such responsibility entails.

In situations wherein we experience unhealthy fear, we need to stop and think. We need to replace our fantasy with reality, with facts and concrete information. We need to replace our wishful thinking with logical thinking and reasoned reflection. Especially in contemporary society do we need to stop the whirl of our lives and examine frequently where our stress, our anxiety, and our feelings of being trapped are coming from. We need to address our fear, dialogue with it, and convert its energies into creative solutions for our lives. Maintaining the tension between healthy and unhealthy fear is one of the adult tasks of our lives. How do we choose to deal creatively with the *real* crises, dangers, or evils in our lives? How do we choose to deal creatively with the *imagined* crises, dangers, or evils in our lives?

Some of us experience the peak of fear *before* the crisis, the danger, or the evil is upon us. Others experience the peak of fear either *during* the crisis or danger, or *after* we have struggled through a crisis, danger, or evil situation. We then experience guilt-fear — the fear that we have not behaved or performed as well as we needed to.

The human feeling or emotion which the Scriptures confront and address most frequently is fear — both healthy and unhealthy fear. One of the basic themes of the Scriptures which precipitate both healthy and unhealthy fear within us is our participation in the Election, the Mission, and the Presence Promise or Blessing from our God. We fear the call, we fear being sent, and we fear that the promise will not be honored by God. Jesus was well aware of the wellsprings of healthy and unhealthy fear deeply buried within us. He knew and understood them both. "Fear not!" "Do not be anxious!" and "Do not be afraid!" were his frequently reiterated responses to women and men who were crippled by their fear. He promised not to leave his followers and his friends orphans. He would send them and us his Spirit, and this he did. The Spirit, our Comforter and our Consoler, is with us in the multiple crises, dangers, or evil situations which we encounter in our lives. The special gifts which the Spirit shares with us are hope and courage. Hope enables us to expect and to depend upon the power and strength of the Spirit within us during our moments of fear. Courage enables us to mobilize our resources and continue our journey through the crisis and the danger. Frequent reflective prayer and meditation enable us to surface our fear, and to summon the energies of the Spirit within us to shrink and to tame it.

SEVEN

Fear Imaging And Faith Imaging

INTRODUCTION

THE BASIC AND CENTRAL MESSAGE of the Good News of Jesus Christ is a message addressed to us regarding fear. "Do *not* be afraid! I am *with* you!" This promise of the Risen Lord's active presence in our lives is the radical message of the Christian Scriptures. In believing and accepting the reality of the Presence Promise, we reframe our perception of ourselves, of others, and of our relationship with *Abba*-God. No longer are we really alone, unattended, and going-it-alone in a threatening, dangerous world. We begin to trust and to rely upon our *inner* resources, the God-given beauty, power, and vision within us. The Spirit enables us to live within the reality of who we are — graced persons who are intimates of the Spirit. As we affirm our own graced personhood, our perception of others is also transformed. They, too, are people of inner beauty, power, and vision. They, too, are struggling with their own healthy and unhealthy fear. They also need to name and claim their radically graced personhood. We need not appeal so much to their good will or favor as to their Spirit-filled goodness in our relationship with them. Jurgen Moltmann enlarges upon this process of love which summons and reaches out to a different and difficult other with "inspired" (motivated by the Spirit) movements of hope, intelligence, and creative caring. He writes, "Whoever repays evil with good must be really free and strong. Love for the enemy does not mean surrendering to the enemy, submission to the enemy's will. Rather, such a person is no longer in the stance of reacting to the enemy, but seeks to create something new, a new situation for the enemy and for herself or himself. Such a person follows her or his own intention and no longer allows the law of actions to be prescribed by the foe" (*On Human Dignity*, p. 126). We need to appeal to the God-given power, beauty, and vision which lies deep within even different and difficult others.

THREE ISSUES OF FEAR

THERE ARE THREE EXPERIENCES OF FEAR which initially were healthy but through the years have become decidedly otherwise in terms of the power that we adults have given to these issues to intimidate and to threaten us. Our imagination can create more personal crises and danger than the reality of a situation actually warrants. The first issue or experience of fear is *separation anxiety*. We fear to be and to become the individual, singular and unique, whom we have been created to be and to become. Most infants experience this discomfort of maternal separation within the first year of their lives; it can recur in acute form when they have to enter school for the first time. When I taught in the elementary parochial schools for ten years, I observed that the first week was always an ordeal for us because of the commotion some of the kindergarten children caused upon leaving their mothers. Some of them cried, screamed, kicked, and became quite hostile. Not only were they a disturbance to the teacher, but they managed to disturb, stimulate, and precipitate similar disruptive behavior in the other children who were not originally upset. The whole class could become a mass of weeping and wailing youngsters. Needless to say, some of the mothers were even more upset than their anxiety-ridden children. Later in our lives separation anxiety assumes more subtle forms of expression. The fear of being alone, of being separated from, or abandoned by those who nurture and care for us can become a quite unhealthy fear in our lives. Many of us prefer to be part of and to participate unobtrusively in groups, and to be lost in the crowd rather than to stand up and speak out on our own. We fear that asserting our own convictions and choices may separate us from the group. It is easier to go-along-with the crowd. We prefer to live as a shrub rather than as an individual tree. We would rather parrot the slogans, the myths, and the sayings of others than communicate our own responses to the realities of our day.

The distance and space which intimacy requires is very painful and uncomfortable for those of us who are prone to separation anxiety. Each of us needs both distance and space in order to reach out and touch others in intimacy and then to welcome the outreach and touch of others in intimacy. The big I (intimacy) demands the big D (distance). Jerry Greenwald describes people who are afraid of creative intimacy with themselves or with others (*Creative Intimacy*, pp. 17-69). He writes,

> Many people spend their lives attempting to free themselves from their lack of self-acceptance and self-love by struggling to achieve recognition from others. Such endeavors rarely change their inner feelings even when they are 'successful' and recognized by others. These people still do not accept themselves as they are and — no matter what respect or praise they receive from others — still do not like themselves (p. 43).

In reaching out to another for intimacy in order to share (not to demand or to grasp) love and life, we have to be rooted in ourselves and at a distance from the other. No two oak trees can afford to be planted too close together. The one would smother the other. Each of us has to be rooted in our own individuality before we can effectively reach out to others. The Scriptures reflect the necessary tension between distance and intimacy which each of us has to cope with. Many of the election moments in Scripture occur when the person called was alone and in seclusion. These people were touched by God during their moments of solitude. We also can expect the Spirit to speak to us in our seclusion. We are also touched by God in our moments of solitude. In such moments we are healed; in such moments we are strengthened; in such moments we are inspired; in such moments we are confronted and challenged.

Some of us adult Christians have an unhealthy fear regarding moments of solitude and seclusion. We are afraid to be alone, to be with ourselves, to be with the Spirit of God who dwells within us. We are like children who are afraid to go down into the basement without someone with us. We imagine all kinds of demons, creeping and crawling creatures, and boogie men awaiting us down there in the dark. Unhealthy fear! Separation anxiety! As adults we have to encounter numerous moments of isolation, seclusion and genuine solitude. Our birth and death occur in moments of isolation. Our moments of reflective decision must take place when we are alone and in solitude. In solitude we establish intimacy with ourselves and dialogue with our spirit. We establish contact and communicate best with ourselves in solitude. We name and claim an intimate relationship with ourselves. We cannot be mature adults until we have experienced intimacy with ourselves, with the Spirit deep within us.

I like to use the analogy of a house for the human person. The attic contains our past. Many of us spend most of our lives rummaging about in the attic reviewing and reliving the events of the past, especially the painful and hurtful situations of our lives. We have albums filled with the black-stamp collection of bygone days upon which we pour out all of our energy, interest, and time. We refuse to let go, to separate ourselves from these past injuries and injustices. The first floor of the house is the present, the reality of our life situation now. We interact with others in a realistic and truthful manner in managing our lives and in fulfilling our responsibilities. The major portion of our energy, interest, and time takes place on the first floor. And then there is the basement. It contains our vision for the future. We descend into the basement to fire up the vision, to generate the power and receive the strength to go about creative and mature living. Basements generally contain the "generators" of the house, e.g., the boiler for generating heat, the air conditioner to cool the house, the electrical system, the telephone connections, and the major plumbing pipes and lines. We need to keep in touch with what is going on in the basement of our being. We need to check frequently to discern if our switches are "On" and working well. So it is that the house of our psyche, our personhood, has three major areas which invite us to be present to them in varying degrees and moments. The inner areas of the attic, the ground floor, and the basement require our time and our attention especially for mature, adult living. Moreover, we adults need to touch base with our past (the attic) as well as our future (the basement) if we are to handle our present (the ground floor) with focus and direction.

    A second issue or experience of fear which develops into unhealthy fear at times is the fear of what *other people think of us*. Our fear of disapproval and our desire for approval are in reality control issues. Some of us are willing to trade in and sell out our own individuality in order to obtain the approval and to avoid the disapproval of others. We are controlled by fear when it comes to others. We surrender our own preferences and our own insights in favor of the selections and opinions of others. We fear their disapproval, and we seek their O.K. They control us and determine the course of our lives. Like Esau, we sell out our birthright of God-given individuality for the hunger-satisfying stew of approval. Like Esau, we care little for the birthright of our individual human dignity and worth (Genesis 26:27-34). Other people control and determine what we do, how we "should" do it, and when it is to be done. In such instances we surrender our human dignity and our human personhood in terms of insight, judgment, and choices. Our unhealthy fear of disapproval also enables us to avoid having to accept the consequences of our own choices and decisions. We reduce ourselves to a childish existence, a fear-filled existence, a robot existence, a puppet existence under the control and power of others. We need to draw upon our own inner resources and inner beauty and power. We need to remember that we are fashioned by *Abba*-God, saved and freed by Christ Jesus, and that we have the energy and the power of the Spirit within us waiting for us to summon them into focus and action. The Spirit is with us! Our sin is our denial of this presence, this power within us. We repeatedly deny our divine identity and relationship.

Some of us live our adult lives in the clutches of a third issue of fear — the unhealthy fear of *hurting someone*. We are afraid to deal well with a given situation because we are afraid that we may hurt a loved one. We do not speak the truth to others for fear we will hurt them. In reality this fear of hurting others is a subtle form of dreading another's disapproval. We are afraid that the person will not like to hear what we need to say. Again, their disapproval commits us to silence or to lies. We also need to be aware that hurt and harm are very different realities. Hurt refers to the discomfort and pain which we experience from another. Hurt is primarily a wound to our self-concept, to our self-image. Our ego (pride) is injured, depleted, or punctured — we lose some of the air in our pride-filled balloon. All of us who relate in a meaningful manner with others can expect to be hurt by them at given moments in our relationship. Our egos do reach out beyond the boundary of reality in terms of what we believe we can be and do in our interactions with others. We get carried away. In very deep and loving relationships there are times when we disappoint others, annoy them, expect too much from them, disagree with and misunderstand them. Such moments hurt us and also hurt others. Yet we do not *harm* them, though we can hurt them deeply. Central to being wounded by another is our *reaction* to being wounded. A wound is a wound is a wound. Yet we often add our own insult to the injury from another thereby precipitating infection, more loss of blood, and even malignancy within the wound. Moreover, we do not summon forth our own inner healing powers and energies. Our self-depreciating or self-destructive response to hurt from others then precipitates and engenders harm. Others hurt us; we harm ourselves. The same process is operative for others. Yes, we may hurt others; however, they and their response to our wrongdoing bring about the harm in their lives. Our inner spirit is our sacred sanctuary and only we are capable of doing harm within the privileged precincts of our personhood. Only we can do harm unto ourselves. We hurt others, yet we do not harm their spirit, the persons whom they are. There are times when we as adults need to confront the people we love with the truth of our convictions and the truth of our response to their behavior which may be consistently destructive. The "Intervention" process in numerous detoxification centers around the country bears ample witness to the necessity to speak the truth in and with love. Failure to speak the truth is more harmful and unloving than confronting with care and concern a family member, friend, or colleague. We act as mature, adult Christians when we are able both to confront and to comfort others in a loving and caring manner. The ability to share truth with and in love is the hallmark of a mature, adult Christian spirituality. We also need to be able to hear the truth spoken with love to us. Speaking and hearing the truth in love creates mutuality, genuine intimacy, and mature Christian community among us.

Christian hope and courage are the gifts with which the Spirit endows us in our day-by-day lives. We continually need to stir up these gifts within us. Obviously, our Christian call invites us to choose life, to choose love — love of self and love of others. Gospel love is fashioned and determined by the use of the Spirit's gifts of hope and courage. What our culture calls love is in many instances condescending pity and ego-serving indulgence. So much need of approval and fear of disapproval function within the image of so-called "love" which culture clings to and recommends. The Christian Scriptures tell us that love casts out fear; Gospel love is a freeing and a healing reality.

FEAR IMAGING

OUR IMAGINATION is one of the most powerful human gifts with which we are endowed. In some ways imagination is THE God-like quality of our human personhood. Without too much effort we can leap back centuries and be present to the building of the Egyptian pyramids, to the assassination of Julius Caesar, or to the infant Moses being found by the princess amid the bullrushes in the river. It is remarkable how we can scan tremendous spans of time and bring them into our present awareness and consciousness. Moreover, a similar process is also true in relation to the future. With our imagination we can project ourselves and others into future scenes and visualize our lives many years hence. Our present state of mind can be altered and reframed in and through our imagination, through visualizing negative or positive scenes or situations.

Transcendental meditation or creative visualization is employed by many women and men to relieve the stress and pressure inherent in their careers. At such times, people assume a relaxed posture, block out and let go of their harried and stress-filled awareness, and then visualize themselves within a peaceful environment — a lakeside, a mountain scene, or a wooded expanse somewhere in a country setting. They position themselves in the visualization and then proceed to draw calm from the peaceful scene. They imagine themselves enjoying the sights, the sounds, the smells, even the touch of a cool breeze upon them. Such a journey into and with the imagination changes their mind-set and their mood. They emerge from the meditation or visualization refreshed and renewed and ready to resume the tasks at hand with greater peace, more focus, and added concentration. Truly a remarkable phenomenon! A minor miracle? No and yes. On the one hand, we humans possess unusual abilities to control and to change our lives at any given moment, so this "miracle" is part of the potential of our personhood. And on the other hand, we find it difficult to accept the powers we have and to use them to function in a full, complete, and free manner. Most of us adults are far more aware of our limitations (self-imposed) than we are of our tremendous capabilities. Our fear — healthy and unhealthy — is the major reason why we fail to actualize much of our human potential. Our fear commits us to a state of ignorance or denial regarding what is genuinely possible for us. Our imagination is the seed-bed of our future. It cradles, nurtures, and enlivens what we can be and become.

Many of us sow bad seed into the ground of our being; then we reap what we have sown. Bad seed is the negative and fear-filled seminal images that we have formed and continue to form of ourselves and of the future of our lives. Deep within us, self-doubt and self-loathing set down roots. Where did we obtain this bad seed? For many of us both our early family life and our years in school contributed to the early formation of the negative self-image which we use for seed. Many of us were told innumerable times about our faults and failings during childhood both within the family and in school. Seldom were we told about our gifts and encouraged and affirmed when we used them well. Our gifts and good behavior were taken for granted. I remember as a youngster I was always being corrected both at home and in school for talking too much. I asked too many questions, and I made too many comments about what I saw and heard. I have to admit that the corrections did not deter me. There were times during the evening family meal when I was silenced because I was doing so much talking. (Never did I anticipate that I would spend years in silence at meals in the convent!) Today I am an effective public speaker. Public speaking has never been a major source of fear for me. And yet when I was in my formative years, my speaking out was considered a wrong, a weakness, and definitely an annoyance. Adulthood has shown me that articulation is one of my gifts. Some of us are afraid to move into new and different ventures because we have received disapproval regarding them or we have been told that we are not capable of achieving them. Others have determined for us what our gifts and abilities are. And we meekly accept their evaluation. In a real sense we determine who we are and what we are capable of achieving through the vision and desires functioning deep inside us. Some of us

Fear Imaging and Faith Imaging

adults have to renew, reframe, and reform our image of who we are and what we can do and become. We program our own lives. We are strongly influential in creating our future. In *Creative Visualization*, Shakti Gawain writes,

> . . . we always attract into our lives whatever we think about the most, believe in most strongly, expect on the deepest level, and/or imagine most vividly.
>
> When we are negative and fearful, insecure or anxious we will tend to attract the very experiences, situations, or people that we are seeking to avoid. If we are basically positive in attitude, expecting and envisioning pleasure, satisfaction, and happiness, we will attract and create people, situations, and events which conform to our positive expectations. . . . (The process of change) involves exploring, discovering, and changing our deepest, most basic attitudes toward life. . . . In the process (creative visualization) we often discover ways in which we have been holding ourselves back, blocking ourselves from achieving satisfaction and fulfillment in life through our fears and negative concepts (p. 7).

Many of us repeatedly, wishfully, and wistfully dream of better days, days of peace and joy, and yet mere wishing and positive thinking are insufficient. The positive images deep within our seed bed, our secret recesses, need to be energized and brought into focus and direction for incorporation into our vision and choices. We need to provide space and scope for the Spirit within us to groan for fullness, for abundance, for quality of life, and for genuine peace and joy.

FAITH IMAGING

FAITH IS AN EMBRACING ATTITUDE, a welcoming posture, a caring position or stance toward life. In and through faith we place ourselves in an accepting posture in relation to ourselves, to others, and to God. Our full personhood assumes the stance of faith. The position or posture we assume reveals a radically true perception of who we are in relation to ourselves and others. Faith is a wholistic posture and attitude. This posture and attitude, rooted as it is in the deepest recesses of our humanity, structures and influences both our intellectual and decision-making processes. Some of us confuse faith with a belief-system, doctrine, or dogma. In contrast to posturing ourselves in faith, we also adhere to belief-systems, doctrines, or dogmas which are theoretical formulations or systematized expressions of our experience of ourselves, of others, and of God. As adults we frequently encounter the belief systems, dogmas, and doctrines which other people adhere to because of their own experience or because they subscribe to the reliability of others. During childhood we depended upon others for our faith in ourselves, in others, and also in God. We may have been told that Mrs. Jones who lived on our block was a sickly lady and we had to be polite to her. Yet we experienced her as a mean, crabby, and bossy woman. She complained when we played near her home, and ran us off when we became too noisy. She didn't like us, and we knew it. Later on we no longer depended upon our parents for an evaluation of her. We formulated our own opinions and called her a few choice names. Our own expressions about Mrs. Jones were in harmony with our experiences of her. Moreover, our experiences and expressions regarding her may or may not have been in agreement with older people's experiences of her. Faith is the response to life which surfaces primarily from our personal experience of life. For us adults the life of faith is a paradox; our life is a mixture of both faith and doubt. In doubt we encounter and experience periodically the *nothingness* of ourselves, of others, and of God. We question the experiential meaning and value of ourselves, of others, and of God. We perceive our lives as meaningless and lacking any significance. In such instances we survey the formless wasteland and dark abyss of our own world and admit the nothingness within its void. In a very real sense we are in a posture of crisis, of opportunity. We possess the opportunity to choose. We can choose to distance ourselves and to curse the darkness, or we can choose to experience the darkness and to call forth the light of a creative solution. Faith is believing ourselves into being; faith is believing others into being, especially when we or they are experiencing self-doubt — darkness and a void.

Faith is creative energy and creative movement. The winds of faith and of creative choice energize and move us to another position, a different posture and stance. The winds of faith contain and carry creative seed for the ground of our being and doing. The winds of faith, the Autumn winds, initiate the transformation of the void and the vacuum within our wasteland world. We encounter and engage nothingness and the death-like void, and we emerge with everything being possible and with new life and energy. Truly a creative God-like posture and process! Dorothee Soelle and Shirley Cloyes encourage us to confront the nothingness within ourselves which threatens to destroy our personhood. These two women assert that in the confrontation with the nothingness within our humanity we participate in the co-creative activity of God (*To Work and to Love*, pp. 38-52). We adults who participate in co-creation are summoned to encounter and to engage the nothingness which both dwells within us and also surrounds us. We participate in the posture and the position of God in relation to this nothingness. Similarly, created in the image of God, we participate in the creative action and energy of God. Moreover, we also encounter and engage the nothingness within the chaos of our lives with creative and innovative consequences. What does it mean to have faith, to believe? To have faith means that we choose to embrace with care and concern the void, the abyss, and the wasteland within ourselves and others. We choose to care for the cavern or the canyon of nothingness rather than damn its darkness and curse its emptiness. Our courageous and creative caring in the midst of the experience of nothingness calls forth the winds of change which carry the seed of life both for ourselves and for others.

A mature faith-posture makes it possible for us to reverence and to cherish ourselves and our lives. A mature faith-stance provides us with the horizons which enable us to realize that *all* of life is sacred — emptiness and fullness, darkness and light, nothing and everything, death and life. Mature faith places us in a posture of welcoming and embracing ourselves and our lives, both the delightful and difficult moments of our journey. A saying of John of the Cross has been very important for me in managing my life: "Where there is no love, put love, and you will find love." He invites us to live creatively, to bring life into the void or vacuum, to function in and with faith. To live with mature faith is to take a stance of care and concern, to be hospitable in the deepest sense of the word, to provide the caring space and soothing salves which renew and refresh ourselves and others. A mature faith-embrace defies and disarms the rigid cynicism and stolid resistance of culture. A mature faith-concern makes fertile the barren and severe wilderness and also makes tender and gentle the harshness within ourselves and others. A mature faith-vision brings light and sight to others who are blinded by the darkness of fear, bias, or ignorance. Self-doubt is diminished, and self-hatred is diluted in the caring and creative presence of a faith posture. In reality faith is love-energy in action, love-energy in motion, love-energy shared with others and welcomed from others. Mature faith delights in the unseen and unappreciated beauty and power within ourselves and others. A mature faith-vision penetrates through the opaque wrappings of ourselves and others and cherishes the beauty and potential (usually hidden and unperceived) of the gift within the package. A mature faith-embrace welcomes the different and the difficult with peace and joy; we offer others a hospitable, open, and life-giving spirit.

FAITH IMAGING AND SACRED SCRIPTURE

THE SCRIPTURES, both Hebrew and Christian, are rooted and centered on women's and men's struggle with faith. The Scriptures detail both the experience and the expression of how women and men have related in faith to God, to others, and to themselves. The Scriptures reveal above all the Lord's relationship with the women and men he has created. The God of the Scriptures is faithful. The Lord God creates and shares life with his people. Mutuality between Yahweh and his people is central to God's covenant with his own: "You will be my people and I will be your God." When Yahweh's people respond in faith, things go well for them. When they give in to doubt and infidelity, they encounter multiple dangerous and evil situations which overwhelm and conquer them. The history of the relationship between Yahweh and his people is a cyclic process of God's extending and establishing the covenant, followed by Israel's infidelity, subsequent destruction, and ensuing remorse. Eventually Israel's remorse leads to Yahweh's mercy and forgiveness, Israel's reconciliation with Yahweh, restoration to integrity and fullness, and then the cycle begins again. The Israelites' faith in God determines their perception of themselves, their stance toward others, and the decisions and choices of their lives.

When their faith-posture was solid and firm, they experienced the abundance of creative lives. When they lost their firm footing and faltered in infidelity, they became self-destructive and miserable. They did not keep the faith in their relationship with Yahweh. As a result, they subsequently lost faith in themselves and in others. Over and over again Yahweh stepped in, reached out, and rescued them from the consequences of their folly and their infidelity.

The two central images of Yahweh's relationship with his people found in the Scriptures are the images of an attentive and faithful shepherd with his flock and the enduring and faithful love between a husband and a wife. Ezekiel describes the shepherding posture of Yahweh when he writes,

> For thus says the Lord God: I myself will look after and tend my sheep. As a shepherd tends his flock when he finds himself among his scattered sheep, so will I tend my sheep. I will rescue them from every place where they were scattered when it was cloudy and dark. I will lead them out from among the peoples and gather them from the foreign lands; I will bring them back to their own country and pasture them upon the mountain of Israel (in the land's ravines and all its inhabited places). In good pastures will I pasture them, and on the mountain heights of Israel shall be their grazing ground. There they shall lie down on good grazing ground, and in rich pastures shall they be pastured on the mountains of Israel. I myself will pasture my sheep; I myself will give them rest, says the Lord God. The lost I will seek out, the strayed I will bring back, the injured I will bind up, the sick I will heal (but the sleek and strong I will destroy), shepherding them rightly (Ezk 34:11-16).

And in the Book of Hosea Yahweh could not renounce Israel who has been unfaithful to him. The passage reads,

Fear Imaging and Faith Imaging

So I will allure her;
    I will lead her into the desert
    and speak to her heart.
From there I will give her the vineyard she had,
    and the valley of Achor as a door of hope.
She shall respond there as in the days of her youth,
    when she came up from the land of Egypt.
On that day, says the Lord,
She shall call me "My husband,"
    and never again "My baal...."
I will espouse you to me forever:
    I will espouse you in right and in justice,
    in love and in mercy;
I will espouse you in fidelity,
    and you shall know the Lord (Ho 2:16-19, 21-22).

Jesus affirmed the importance of faith in his encounters with the women and men in his ministry. His faith in his Father was certainly solid and firm. He realized and welcomed his Father's favor and spent his life communicating to others that they also were pleasing to the Father, were favored by the Father, were loved by the Father. He summoned others to stand solidly and firmly in a posture of faith toward *Abba*-God, themselves, and others. He invited his friends and followers to allow him to transform their perception and experience of themselves from a posture of fear to a posture of faith. He invited them to perceive themselves in the reality of being and acting as children of *Abba*-God and as sisters and brothers to each other. Jesus called his followers and his friends to conversion in terms of their consciousness and their conduct. He also calls us to such a conversion of consciousness and conduct. Energized and empowered by the Spirit within us, we need to remember who we are in relation to our radical identity in *Abba*-God and in our relationship with ourselves and with others. The Spirit within us vitalizes and solidifies our posture and our position of faith in relation to ourselves and to others. Frequently we need to summon from within us the energy and power of the Spirit in order to enable us to assume the solid and firm posture of mature, adult faith.

SUMMARY

THERE ARE THREE ISSUES OR EXPERIENCES of fear which become unhealthy in terms of the power we adults have given to these experiences to intimidate and threaten us. The first is separation anxiety. We fear to be and to become the individual, singular and unique, whom we have been created to be and to become. We fear to function with our own conviction and commitment in the choices which our lives demand of us. Instead, we choose to parrot the slogans and sayings of others rather than communicate our own responses to the realities of our lives. Each of us needs both distance and space from others in order to reach out and touch others in intimacy. Each of us has to be rooted within our own individuality in order to extend and reach out to others. As adults we have to encounter numerous moments of aloneness, moments of genuine solitude. Many of us are uncomfortable during these times of solitude and seclusion. We need to name and to claim an intimate relationship with ourselves, which genuine aloneness and solitude engender. Within the house of selfhood, we need to be present as adults to our past (the attic) as well as to our future (the basement) if we are to manage our present (the ground floor) with focus and direction.

Another fear-related issue which becomes unhealthy for adults is the fear of what other people think of us. Our fear of disapproval and our desire for approval are in reality control

Fear Imaging and Faith Imaging

issues. We are controlled by our desire for approval of others and by our fear of their disapproval. Others control us and determine the course of our lives. In such instances we surrender our human dignity and our human personhood in that we relinquish our own insight, judgment, and choices in given situations.

Some of us live our adult lives in the clutches of a third fear-related issue — the fear of hurting someone. In reality this fear of hurting others is a subtle form of dreading another's disapproval. We are afraid that others will not like to see or hear what we need to do or say to them. Our fear of their disapproval commits us to silence or to untruth. Hurt and harm are two different realities. Hurt refers to the discomfort, the pain, and the suffering which we experience from another's behavior. Our sense of self is depreciated, deflated, and depleted in the experience. Harm is the additional injury which we inflict upon ourselves when we are hurt or wounded by others. Harm is self-abuse, self-destruction, self-rejection and negation. Others hurt us; we harm ourselves. Our inner self is a sacred sanctuary; we alone are capable of inflicting harm therein. We act as mature adults when we are able to confront and to comfort others in a loving and caring manner. The ability to share the truth with and in love is the hallmark of mature, adult Christian spirituality. We also need to be able to hear and accept the truth spoken by others with love to us. Speaking and hearing the truth in love creates mutuality, genuine intimacy, and mature Christian community among us.

Our imagination is one of the most powerful and innovative forces and human gifts with which we are endowed. It possesses a divine-like energy and potential. It enables us to control and to change our lives at any chosen moment. And yet we find it difficult to make it work for us to our advantage. Our imagination is the seed-bed of our future. It cradles, nurtures, and enlivens in us what we can become. Many of us sow bad seed into the ground of our being; then we reap what we have sown. Bad seed engenders the negative and fear-filled seminal images that we have formed and continue to form of ourselves and of our future. Many of us need new and good seed to sow within the ground of our being. Some of us have to renew, reframe, and reform the image of who we are and what we can become and do with our lives. The positive images of faith buried deep within our secret recesses need to be energized and brought into focus and direction for incorporation into our vision and choices for the future.

Faith is an all-embracing attitude, a welcoming posture, a caring position toward life. In and through faith we take our stand in relation to ourselves, to others, and to God. This posture or attitude, rooted as it is in the deepest recesses of our humanity, structures and influences both our intellectual and decision-making processes. Some of us confuse faith with a belief-system, doctrine, or dogma. Faith is a response to life surfacing primarily from our personal experience of life. For us adults the life of faith is a mixture of both faith and doubt. In doubt we encounter and experience periodically the nothingness of ourselves and our lives. In doubt we are put in a posture of discomfort before the darkness of the abyss, the canyon, or the cave of nothingness. We are invited to choose either to curse the dreaded darkness or to surrender with faith to the darkness and subsequently perceive the light within the deep abyss. Faith is believing ourselves into being; faith is believing others into being, especially when we or they are experiencing the doubt of darkness and nothingness. As adults, we are called to participate in creation, and are summoned to encounter and to engage the nothingness which is both within us and which surrounds us. To have faith means to choose to embrace with care and concern the void, the abyss, and the wasteland within ourselves and others. We choose to care for the cavern or the canyon of nothingness rather than damn its darkness and curse its emptiness.

A mature faith-stance provides us with the horizons which enable us to realize that all of life is sacred: emptiness and fullness, darkness and light, nothing and everything, death and life. A mature faith-vision brings light and sight to others who are blinded by the darkness of fear, bias, or ignorance.

The Scriptures record the experience and expression of women and men in their struggle with faith. The Scriptures reveal above all the Lord's posture and relationship with us his people. Yahweh is faithful! Mutuality between Yahweh and his people is central to the convenant-reality contained in Scripture. The Israelites' faith in their God determined their experience of themselves, their attitude toward others, and the decisions and choices of their lives. Over and over again Yahweh reached out and rescued them from the consequences of their folly, their infidelity, and their faithlessness. Jesus affirmed the importance of faith in his encounters with the women and men in his ministry. He invited his friends and his followers to enable him to transform from fear to faith their perception and experience of themselves. He called them and he calls us to conversion in terms of consciousness and conduct. Furthermore, energized and empowered by the Spirit within us, we are made firm and solid in our faith-posture and faith-position in relation to *Abba*-God, ourselves and others.

Bibliography

DONNELLY, DORIS. *Learning to Forgive* (Nashville: Abingdon Press), 1982.
―― *Putting Forgiveness into Practice*, (Argus: Chicago), 1982.
ERIKSON, ERIK. *Identity and the Life Cycle* (New York: W.W. Norton), 1980.
GAWAIN, SHAKTI. *Creative Visualization* (New York: Bantam Books), 1982.
GAYLIN, WILLARD. *Feelings* (New York: Ballantine Books), 1979.
―― *The Rage Within* (New York: Simon and Schuster), 1984.
GREENWALD, JERRY. *Creative Intimacy* (New York: Jove Books), 1975.
JOHNSTON, WILLIAM. *Christian Mysticism Today* (New York: Harper & Row), 1984.
KUBLER-ROSS, ELISABETH. *On Death and Dying* (London: Collier-Macmillan Ltd.), 1969.
LINN, MATTHEW and LINN, DENNIS. *Healing of Memories* (New York: Paulist Press), 1974.
―― *Healing Life's Hurts* (New York: Paulist Press), 1978.
MOLTMANN, JURGEN. *The Crucified God* (New York: Harper & Row), 1974.
―― *On Human Dignity* (Philadelphia: Fortress Press), 1984.

MONTAGU, ASHLEY. *Growing Young* (New York: McGraw-Hill), 1981.

OTTO, RUDOLF. *The Idea of the Holy* (London: Oxford University Press), 1967.

PECK, M. SCOTT. *The Road Less Traveled* (New York: Simon and Schuster), 1978.

——— *People of the Lie* (New York: Simon and Schuster), 1983.

PEGUY, CHARLES. *God Speaks* (New York: Pantheon Books), 1945.

SCHILLEBEECKX, EDWARD. *Christ* (New York: Seabury Press), 1980.

——— *God Is New Each Moment* (New York: Seabury Press), 1983.

SOELLE, DOROTHEE and CLOYES, SHIRLEY A. *To Work and to Love* (Philadelphia: Fortress Press), 1984.